D1519976

The Complete
Guide to
SAILING

A. H. DRUMMOND, JR.

Illustrations by John Fleming
Foreword by George O'Day

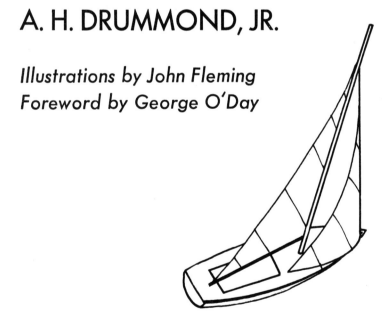

A FIRESIDE BOOK
PUBLISHED BY SIMON & SCHUSTER, INC.
NEW YORK

Copyright © 1971 by Doubleday & Company, Inc.

All rights reserved
including the right of reproduction
in whole or in part in any form

First Fireside Edition 1986
Published by Simon & Schuster, Inc.
Simon & Schuster Building
Rockefeller Center
1230 Avenue of the Americas
New York, New York 10020

Published by arrangement with Doubleday & Company, Inc.
FIRESIDE and colophon are registered trademarks of Simon & Schuster, Inc.
Manufactured in the United States of America

1   2   3   4   5   6   7   8   9   10

Library of Congress Cataloging in Publication Data

ISBN: 0-671-63207-8

This book is dedicated to my wife Anne,
for without her enthusiasm for sailing,
it might never have been written.

Foreword

With the growing competition for man's leisure time, sailing is the one sport that seems to be able to involve the entire family. To sail on a pond, a lake, an ocean, or even a large swimming pool, is relaxation and enjoyment of the highest order. What holds back families from enjoying this sport is the mystique that seems to surround the sport itself. People seem to be afraid to sail. They are afraid to try it; the water terrifies them. Most of this fear is unfounded. Thus, the main job, in order to get people to enjoy sailing, is to get them to try it.

A power boat is different. Here people understand the switch that turns the engine on, the steering wheel, the accelerator, and the gears. Once they hear the power, they are able to put the boat into forward or reverse and take off across the water. Perhaps some are foolhardy and careless, but as in a car, they are driving and they are in control. This, to some people, means fun. After a while, however, driving a power boat becomes as tedious as driving a car. There is little enjoyment. There is no peace of mind, and one must constantly be on the watch for dangers that may lurk ahead. None of this is true with sailing. While sailing you can have peace of mind. You are not going fast, and you are enjoying the elements as they come to you. The wind and the water are challenges that man has been striving to conquer since time began.

As one of our Presidents commented when he tried a sailboat for the first time, "Why hadn't I tried this before? It is relaxing—there is no noise, and there is a feeling of peace around you."

Sailing is this—and much more—if you will only get out and try it.

Bringing the joys of sailing to the adult world is one of the toughest jobs we have. We must educate and explain; the natural fear that older people feel is something that we must conquer. Children take to sailing practically at the first exposure, but people from twenty and up are very reluctant to get started. Whether this is from not wanting to be shown up by the children, or just a case of shyness and reluctance, is a question that I cannot answer.

In the sailing schools that we conduct we find that only about one out of twenty people have ever tried sailboats. And yet, by the time we are finished teaching the people to sail and exposing them to the water, over one-third end up buying sailboats of their own. The others would buy, but they have not yet saved up enough money to get that first boat. In this particular sailing school, we have questioned many people, and have found that 90 percent who come to the school would not have tried sailing in the first place, except that it was required sales training in conjunction with a major chain's selling effort.

Besides getting the newcomers onto the water, there has to be some other means of explaining sailboating to the novice; this is through beginner's books. Good basic books on sailing are rare. Most books start out in the first chapter on basics, and then very quickly launch into phases of sailing that the newcomer finds well over his head. This, of course, baffles him. Once he sees the complexities of the sport, he drops the book and becomes a believer that there is a mystique that he will never learn. These books deal with apparent wind angles, keel angles, vectors, and other complications far too difficult for someone looking for basic information. This is not the case with "Lee" Drummond, who is one of the rare experts on sailing who can treat the subject in a basic manner. He writes so that you can understand sailing. He writes with ease and uses a minimum of technical vocabulary. His basic approach is sound and it is complete.

The Complete Beginner's Guide to Sailing is a delightful textbook of information. You can read it like a novel, and be taken through a very orderly, sensible pattern of lessons that help you understand what to do on the water. When you finish the book you should be ready to move into the more complicated aspects of the sport, such as racing, blue water cruising, and perhaps even surfing with your sailboat.

If you learn to sail, you and your family have a lifetime of enjoyment ahead. The sport gives back to you exactly what you put into it. The challenge is constantly there, because to date no one has conquered the wind and the sea.

GEORGE O'DAY

Acknowledgments

I wish to extend special appreciation to John Fleming, George Erswell, Bruce White, and Louis Vaczek—sailors all—for their careful reading of the manuscript of *The Complete Beginner's Guide to Sailing,* and for their many helpful suggestions and criticisms. I am also indebted to Dorothy Sondin for her help with the voluminous correspondence that accompanied development of the manuscript, and to my wife Anne for typing the manuscript.

Contents

The Complete Guide to Sailing

1. Recognizing Sailboats

". . . once the sailor drops his mooring lines or hoists his anchor, he is cut off from the world of men and makes a world of his own . . ."*
Thus it is with the boys, girls, men, and women who have discovered the thrills of sailing, who have felt the vibrant life of a sailboat perfectly tuned to wind and water. The true sailor inhales the fresh wind with deep satisfaction upon casting off, feeling just as ancient seafaring men must have felt as they faced the unknown oceans. Every sailing trip, be it short or long, on a river, lake, or ocean, is an adventure in its own right. The sailor steers his vessel into the elements each new time confident that he will be challenged, but also knowing that the experience will be both refreshing and renewing. With a hand on the tiller, and the rest of his body acutely attuned to the boat and the forces acting on it, the sailor is truly master of a world in miniature.

You can be that sailor. Sailing is one of the most satisfying recreational activities known. But it is a sport that has to be learned. You don't just hop into a sailboat and sail away, as those who have tried it have discovered. There is really only one way to learn how to sail, and that is to actually sail a boat. A great deal, however, must be understood before a boat is taken out. That is the purpose of this book.

* Morton Hunt, *The Inland Sea,* Doubleday, 1965.

As you read on, you will discover many important things about sailboats and how they sail. You will learn to recognize the different types of boats that are seen on our waters. From time to time, you will come upon photographs of sailboats that have historical significance. These are included in the book to give you a feeling for America's sailing heritage. You will learn how sailboats are put together, and why they behave the way they do. Very important indeed, you will discover what makes a sailboat go.

As you are well aware, virtually all exciting and rewarding sports carry with them some danger. Sailing is no exception. The careful and well-trained sailor is safer in his boat than he is on the highway in the family car. On the other hand, the careless and uninformed sailor runs many risks. He may find himself caught in a sudden storm, and not know what to do. He may be hit on the head by a flying boom. With the number of different lines there are on a sailboat, he might very well become entangled in a sheet line, a halyard, or the anchor rope. Safety afloat, as you will discover, is an important part of sailing. By first learning how to sail, and then by observing just a few basic rules when you are on the water, you will make sailing a source of lifelong enjoyment.

Men and women well advanced in years still sail and still thrill to the special magic that seems to take place when skipper, boat, wind, and water come together in perfect harmony. *Read on;* the sooner you bend on sail and cast off, the better. Good sailing!

THE TYPES OF SAILBOATS

How many times have you stood on shore gazing at sailboats? If you're like most people, you wanted desperately each time to be out there with the sailors. But on what type of boat? Would your preference be a sloop, a ketch, or a cat boat? Perhaps your innermost desire is to someday skipper a schooner such as the *Bowdoin* (see page 71). Do you remember your first sailboat? When I was a boy, about eight or nine years old, I desperately wanted a sailboat, but couldn't afford one. So I did the next best thing. I built an imaginary boat on top of a high sand dune overlooking the ocean. I outlined a boat about fifteen feet long in the sand, and hollowed out the inside. Then, using a long pole, two pieces of bamboo, and a large square of old canvas, I fashioned a square sail that caught the wind and filled beautifully. I confess that I sat for hours in that sandy "boat," and I know that no sailor ever sailed as many places in as short a time as I did. Despite the many different types of boats I've sailed since then, I'll always remember how thrilled I was when that threadbare old piece of canvas filled and started to pull on the lines in my hands.

What type of rig appeals to you most, the *jib-headed* or *gaff-headed?* Do the words *lateen* or *gunter* mean anything to you? If you are looking closely at sailboats for the first time, many of these terms will seem strange. But they needn't be. Let's begin to learn about

These New England youngsters are "learning the ropes" in Beetle Cats, a popular small cat boat. (Photo by Dorothy I. Crossley)

sailing by taking the mystery out of the different types of boats you will see. After all, when something strange and unusual becomes familiar, it is no longer a mystery. Sailboats, like many other things that seem forbiddingly strange at first, are really not difficult to understand.

Sailboats generally fall into two groups: those that are square-rigged and those that are fore-and-aft rigged. On fore-and-aft-rigged boats the sails are rigged parallel to the keel. The sails of square-riggers, on the other hand, are rigged at right angles to the line of the keel. You have most certainly seen pictures of such square-riggers as barks, brigantines, and clipper ships. In this book we will concern ourselves with fore-and-aft-rigged boats only. Modern sailors prefer the fore-and-aft rig because it sails closer to the wind than square-rigged boats.

The simplest way to classify fore-and-aft-rigged boats is by the number of masts, the position of the masts, and the type of sails carried. Most of the boats you will see and use are single masted. Moreover, most single-masted vessels are sloops. The drawing shows the difference

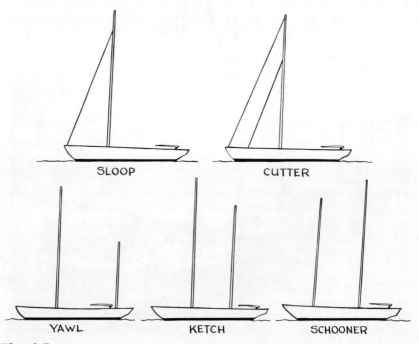

The difference between sloops, cutters, yawls, ketches, and schooners is determined by the number of masts and the position of the masts.

between a *sloop* and a *cutter.* On a cutter the mast is stepped farther aft than on a sloop. (*Aft* is the opposite of *forward.*) This means that the mainsail of a cutter will be smaller than the main of a sloop. In addition, the cutter can carry more than one *headsail* (the sails rigged forward of the mast). In order to be completely accurate, it should be pointed out that the correct name for the boat shown in the diagram is *knockabout.* A true sloop carries a *bowsprit,* and sometimes a projection from the stern called a *boomkin.* Such boats were hard to handle, with so much of the rigging extending forward from the bow and aft from the stern. In the knockabout, which for convenience we will call the sloop, all of the rig is inboard and easy to get at.

Two-masted boats are either *yawls, ketches,* or *schooners,* depending upon placement and height of the masts. On yawls and ketches the smaller mast—the *mizzenmast*—is aft of the taller mast—the *mainmast.* Yawls and ketches are then distinguished by the position of the mizzenmast compared to the position of the *tiller* and *rudder.* On a yawl the mizzenmast is positioned aft of the tiller; it is also quite short compared to the height of the mainmast. On a ketch the mizzenmast is somewhat taller, and it is stepped forward of the tiller. On typical schooners, the shorter of the two masts—the *foremast*—is forward of the mainmast.

Two-masted boats are usually larger than sloops and cutters. They are primarily intended for long-range cruising, and carry two masts in order to break the sail plan down into smaller segments. As you can easily see, any boat sailing great distances away from its own harbor will meet a wide variety of wind and wave conditions. On two-masted craft it is possible to carry more sail in light winds and smooth seas. On the other hand, when the winds are strong and the seas rough, the amount of sail can be easily reduced to a safe level. In rough weather, for example, it is not unusual to see a ketch sailing on the jib and mizzen alone, with the mainsail tightly furled. The sail plan of the schooner is even more flexible. Schooners were originally fishing boats, which required that they sail under wide extremes of weather. The modern schooner, utilizing what the fishing fleets of a hundred years ago learned, carries light-weather and heavy-weather sails in a variety of shapes and sizes. More than any other type of fore-and-aft-rigged vessel, the schooner can match sails to weather for smooth and easy sailing. This is not as simple for a sloop. The mainsail of a sloop must be *reefed* (see the Glossary) in order to

Small sloops such as the Widgeon may be seen wherever there is active interest in sailing. (Photo by O'Day Company)

shorten sail in high winds. Reefing, however, is a difficult task. This is one reason why fewer sloops than yawls and ketches cruise the open oceans for great distances.

THE COMMON SAIL PLANS

By far the most popular sail plan is the *jib-headed* rig. Less popular, but still a familiar sight, is the *gaff-headed* rig. In the early days of sail, using fore and aft rigged boats in this country, the gaff-headed rig was the only one in use. Both pleasure and working boats used it. Two developments then occurred that led to wider and wider use of the jib-headed rig. First, stays that would support the much taller masts needed for jib-headed mainsails were developed. And then it was discovered that the taller jib-headed main was much more efficient as well as easier to handle than the gaff-headed main.

A comparison of the two types will show you why most sailors prefer the jib-headed rig, while some still cling to the gaff-headed sail plan. As the drawing shows, a jib-headed mainsail is very high

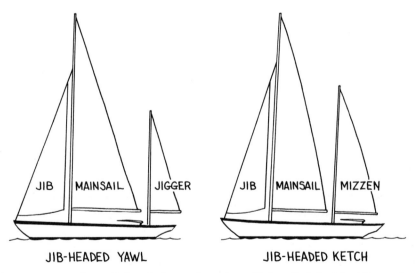

JIB-HEADED YAWL   JIB-HEADED KETCH

Comparison of a jib-headed yawl and a jib-headed ketch. Note that the mizzenmast is forward of the tiller on a ketch. The sail carried by the mizzenmast is the mizzensail on both, although it is popularly called the "jigger" on a yawl.

along the *luff*, the forward part of the sail, and quite short at the *foot*. Just the opposite is true of the gaff-headed main. This type of sail is short along the luff and long at the foot. This difference greatly influences how the boat will sail. You will learn why in Chapter 4. At this point, it is enough to say that jib-headed sails pick up higher breezes, while gaff-headed sails can only pick up surface breezes. In addition, the jib-headed rig generates more drive when sailing to windward (see Glossary), a characteristic much desired by modern skippers.

There are also important differences in the weight of construction of the two types of rig. Gaff-rigged boats are usually of heavy construction, with short, heavy masts, and thick, heavy *shrouds* and *stays* to support the mast and heavy sails. Boats carrying the jib-headed rig, on the other hand, are usually of much lighter, although quite strong, construction. They carry taller, lightweight masts, and thin but

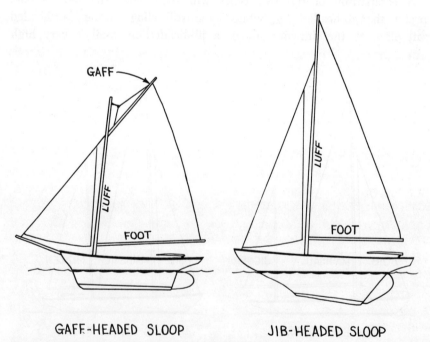

GAFF-HEADED SLOOP   JIB-HEADED SLOOP

Comparison of a jib-headed sloop and a gaff-headed sloop. The gaff rig requires a heavier mast and sturdier shrouds and stays. Note the longer luff and shorter foot on the jib-headed mainsail.

very strong stainless steel shrouds and stays. These differences in weight and construction make for important handling differences. For example, the mainsail of a gaff-headed rig must be raised by two halyards, one at the throat and the other at the peak of the gaff—the spar supporting the top edge of the sail. This usually requires two men, whereas only one man is needed to raise the much lighter jib-headed mainsail.

The drawing also shows two radically different hull types. The hull shown with the gaff-headed rig has a long keel and will steer a straighter course with less effort. This hull also has relatively short overhangs fore and aft, and consequently handles the seas better in rough weather. Both of these characteristics are desirable in boats used for long-distance cruising. The other hull is more suitable for racing and local cruising. It is more easily turned when under way or in the close quarters near a dock, and usually sails better into the wind.

Gaff-headed boats, because of their very large sail area, are usually faster when sailing with the wind at right angles to the boat or coming from aft. When sailing to windward, however, they are not nearly as efficient as jib-headed boats because of the rather short luff on the mainsail. The smaller sail area on a jib-headed boat is a disadvantage when sailing with the wind on the beam or aft of the beam. It was to compensate for this disadvantage that *genoa jibs* and *spinnakers* were developed. More about these interesting types of sail in Chapter 5.

As you look at jib-headed boats, you will notice that the sails on some seem very tall and narrow, while the sails on others seem short and squat. There are reasons for these different shapes. The forward third of the area of the mainsail—the luff—is the part of the sail that generates the most driving force when the boat is sailing to windward, that is, as close into the wind as possible. As you can readily see, the taller the mainsail the longer the luff, or drive area. Thus, the taller the sail the better the boat will sail to windward, all other factors being equal. If two boats carry the same sail area, the one with the taller mast and the taller mainsail is said to have a higher *aspect ratio*. In addition to sailing better to windward, boats with a high aspect ratio do better in protected waters because the tall sails pick up higher breezes. On the other hand, for ocean sailing, when the breezes are close to the surface, a medium aspect ratio is more desirable.

SOME UNUSUAL RIGS

In addition to the frequently seen sloops, yawls, and ketches, you will also spot a variety of unusual rigs on small boats, particularly in and around seaside resort areas and harbors. Some of these are shown in the drawing.

The *gunter* rig is popular for use on small dinghies. As you know, larger cruising sailboats often tow a dinghy along to allow freedom of movement in strange harbors. But all sailboats have a storage problem. There just isn't very much space. Where do you find space for the

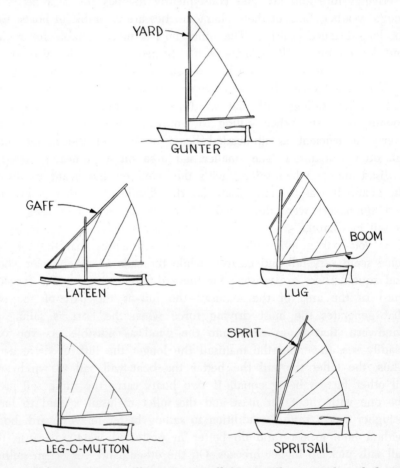

Some of the rigs you will see on small boats. These single-sailed rigs are usually easier to manage on small boats such as dinghies and sailboards.

dinghy spars—the yard, mast, and boom? You don't really want to leave them behind. They are a source of great fun, as anyone knows who has seen the little sailing "dinks" skimming around crowded harbors during the late afternoon and evening hours. The gunter rig solves this problem by permitting storage of the yard, mast, boom, and sails under the seats of the dinghy itself. Thus, everyone gets a chance to sail, and the rig is safely stowed out of the way between harbors.

The *lateen* rig is widely used on the very popular sailboards seen almost everywhere. The hull of these boats resembles a surfboard. The rig consists of a triangular sail with the boom and gaff meeting

Exciting action on Lake Memphremagog in Vermont aboard a Pirate Fish, a typical sailboard. (Photo by M. Wilson)

at the forward point of the triangle. The sail is hoisted obliquely to the mast. Lateen-rigged sailboards are very fast and exciting. They are relatively inexpensive, easy to handle, and quickly righted in the event of a capsize.

Leg-o-mutton is the original term for the jib-headed mainsail. As you can see, it closely resembles the main of a modern jib-headed sloop, although it is longer on the foot. Leg-o-mutton rigs are still popular on small dinghies. To clear up any possible confusion, this is a good point to note that there are two other common names for the jib-headed mainsail—*Marconi* and *Bermudian*.

The *lug*, or *lugger* rig dates back at least to the days of the square-riggers. It was a rig widely used by pirates and smugglers because with it these gentlemen of fortune could outdistance square-riggers by sailing closer to the wind. Not many lug rigs are seen today, although occasionally you will see a dinghy fitted out this way. In addition, some of the Chinese junks seen more and more as pleasure boats carry lug rigs.

If you had been a Dutch settler in old New Amsterdam (New York), you would have had ample opportunity to see *spritsails* in use. In this rig a spar called a sprit extends from the peak of the sail to the *tack*—the point where mast, boom, and sail come together. A few sailboats today carry the spritsail rig, ranging from tiny dinghies all the way up to seventy-foot Thames barges.

2. Sailboat Hulls

You're about to buy your first sailboat, and you face several difficult decisions. You will have to decide on the following at least: size and type of rig; high or low aspect ratio; daggerboard, centerboard, bilge-boards, or keel; self-bailing or open cockpit; round, flat, arc, or V bottom; material of construction—wood, fiberglass, or aluminum. Some of these decisions, of course, will be made in terms of how much you can spend. But despite the amount of money you are willing to spend, others you will have to make in terms of your own judgment. In this chapter we will discuss hulls—the different types, as well as the characteristics of wood, fiberglass, and aluminum for hull construction. In addition, the differences between centerboards and keels will be described.

ROUND, FLAT, OR V BOTTOM

There are just three basic shapes to sailboat hulls—*round, flat,* or *V bottom.* Any other shape on a conventional hull is a variation of these three. This excludes catamaran and trimaran hulls, of course, although any single hull on a multihulled boat would have to be derived from the basic shapes.

In general, the round-bottom hull is more seaworthy than the others. It tends to have an easier motion in all kinds of sea conditions, and performs best of all the hull types when the boat is sailing to windward

Very fast and exciting in a stiff breeze, twin-hulled catamarans such as the DC-14 are gaining in popularity. (Photo by Nancy Smith, courtesy of Duncan Sutphen, Inc.)

into oncoming seas. Under these conditions the round-bottom hull pounds much less, giving an easier and more confortable ride. There is also appearance. Most sailors will tell you they like the way a round-bottom hull looks in the water. As you may have guessed, larger sailboats designed for ocean cruising usually have round bottoms. Many small boats, however, are round bottomed also. If they have a fault, small round-bottom boats are "wetter" than flat- or V-bottom boats. A "wet" boat takes a lot of spray in the cockpit. Much of the fun of sailing is lost when you sit soaking wet with spray in a stiff, cool breeze.

Flat- and V-bottom boats have somewhat different characteristics. As the drawing shows, these boats are said to have *hard chines*. Round-bottom boats have *soft chines*. Hard-chined boats heel less readily in light-to-medium breezes than round-bottom boats of an equivalent size. When a sailboat tips to one side it is said to heel. In addition, when sailing with the wind astern, hard chines have a stabilizing effect that reduces the tendency of the boat to roll, makes steering easier, and cuts down the danger of an accidental jibe. When a boat jibes, the mainsail and boom flip from one side to the other as the wind passes astern. As you can see, if the wind is strong, the rapidly moving boom can be a dangerous weapon.

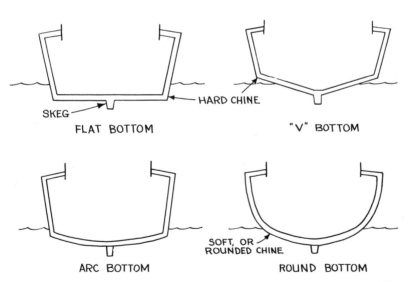

The shapes of flat-, V-, arc-, and round-bottom boats. The different shapes handle differently, making it necessary to choose carefully when buying a boat.

When a boat such as this 420-A sloop is planing it skims over the top of the water at almost double its usual speed. Planing hulls are light in weight and have a relatively flat bottom. (Photo by Grampian Marine, Ltd.)

Flat-bottom hulls are the easiest and most economical to build. They are also the least desirable for sailboat use. V-bottom and arc-bottom hulls are more difficult to construct than flat-bottom hulls, and also more desirable. Many popular small boats have arc and V bottoms. It's interesting to note that with the widespread use of molded fiberglass, more and more small boat hulls are being made with arc- and round-bottom hulls. The forms for a fiberglass hull can be made in any shape desired. Building a round-bottom hull of wood, however, is a tedious, difficult job.

Be sure to take into account local weather conditions when you prepare to buy a sailboat. If you plan to sail in waters that are protected from high winds and heavy seas, a boat with a tall rig, lots of sail area, narrow decks, and low freeboard will give you plenty of sailing excitement with minimum danger. Freeboard is the distance between the water and the edge of the deck. On the other hand, if you will be sailing on unprotected waters that are often rough, you will be better off with a boat having wide decks, generous freeboard, and carrying less sail.

The *stability* of a hull as a sailboat heels is, of course, an important factor. Stability here refers to resistance to heeling. A boat that heels easily in a light breeze is said to be *tender;* it is relatively unstable. The opposite is *stiffness;* a boat that resists heeling is said to be *stiff.* Hard-chined hulls, including the modern planing type dinghy hull, are stiffer than soft-chined hulls, all other factors being equal. The drawing shows the differences between the stability of a hard-chined centerboard boat and a round-bottom fin keel boat. As the hard-chined hull heels, there is a strong buoyant effect on the portion of the hull submerged, tending to right the boat. The centerboard is relatively light in weight, however, and exerts only a small downward force against the direction of heeling. On a keel boat, just the opposite effect occurs. There is little or no buoyant force on the soft-chine "wineglass" hull as the boat heels. The keel is very heavy, however, and as it rises on the side opposite the direction of heel, its weight exerts a strong force that tends to keep the boat upright.

Centerboard boats often capsize in very strong breezes. There just isn't enough countering force opposite the force of the wind pushing the boat over. Well-designed keel boats, on the other hand, are almost impossible to capsize. Moreover, many modern keel boats are designed to right themselves in the unlikely event of a knockdown.

CENTERBOARD VS. KEEL

Keel boats are generally more seaworthy than centerboard boats. As pointed out, this is because the heavy weight of the keel adds stability, making it very difficult to capsize the boat. The added weight of the keel, however, may be a disadvantage. A swamped keel boat will sink unless it is equipped with foam flotation or flotation tanks. Centerboarders, on the other hand, float when they are swamped. This refers, of course, to boats constructed of wood. A swamped fiberglass or aluminum centerboarder will sink unless it is fitted out with flotation materials. A centerboard boat can be made more seaworthy by building it with a wide *beam,* a high *freeboard,* and wide decks. Centerboarders built this way are often more stable and seaworthy than many keel boats.

Most of your sailing will probably be in centerboard boats. Some

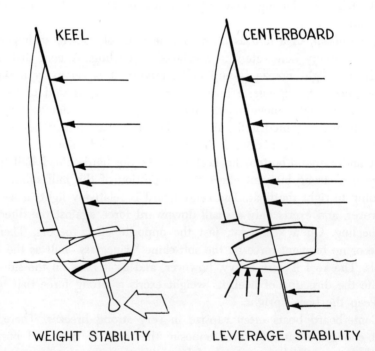

Leverage stability compared to weight stability. In leverage stability, the buoyant effect on the hard chine of the hull is the most important factor. In weight stability, the weight of the keel is the most important factor.

may carry a special form of centerboard called a *daggerboard.* Both centerboard and daggerboard do the same job: They add to stability by providing a small amount of weight low in the water and by leverage; they aid in steering; and finally, they help prevent the boat from slipping sideways when the wind is on the beam or forward of the beam.

As the drawing shows, a daggerboard is long and narrow. It is usually lighter in weight than a centerboard, and is sometimes even cut away in the center to further reduce weight. Daggerboards are slipped straight down into a slotted trunk. Centerboards work differently. They are pivoted at the forward end and hauled by a *pennant* run through a pulley. Because the daggerboard is light in weight it is fairly easy to handle. The daggerboard trunk is narrow and placed well forward, giving more room in the cockpit. A serious disadvantage is that if the daggerboard hits something underwater, both the board and its trunk may be severely damaged. This does not happen with a centerboard,

Heavier hulls with deep keels are called displacement hulls. They literally push the water aside when under way, and will not plane. The hull of this Shields One Design boat is of the displacement type. (Photo by Chris Craft Corporation)

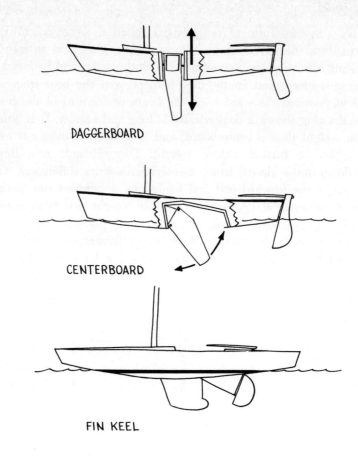

DAGGERBOARD

CENTERBOARD

FIN KEEL

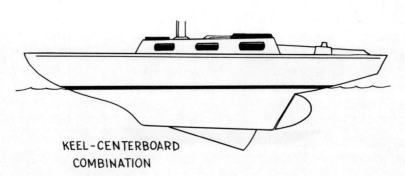

KEEL-CENTERBOARD
COMBINATION

Comparison of daggerboard, centerboard, fin keel, and keel-centerboard combination. Choose the type you prefer in terms of the kind of sailing you expect to do.

for it is free to rotate up and away from any underwater obstacle it may strike.

One great advantage of centerboard and daggerboard boats is that the board's position in the water may be changed to improve the performance of the boat. This is easier with a centerboard, of course, for when a daggerboard is raised it extends up into the cockpit, adding one more object to get in the way of crew and inboard lines. As you watch good skippers in action, particularly when racing, you will see how they frequently adjust the position of the centerboard. The object is to find the best balance among weight distribution, sail setting, centerboard position, and helm to get the best sailing performance.

Different skippers have different ideas about how to adjust the centerboard under similar conditions. Despite these differences, however, it is possible to set out some general rules. Let's consider three situations: *beating*—sailing to windward; *reaching*—when the wind is on the beam; and *running*—when the wind is astern. When beating (see Glossary) to windward, a large portion of the wind's force acts to drive the boat sideways. Thus it is necessary for the centerboard to be lowered all the way to provide maximun lateral resistance to this driving force. The boat heels when beating because the centerboard prevents it from slipping sideways, although it is free to rotate on an axis running along the length of the boat at the waterline. All sailboats slip sideways except when the wind is dead astern. This slippage is called *leeway* (more about leeway later).

When running before the wind (see Glossary), there is no need for lateral resistance. Hence, the centerboard is hauled all the way up. Occasionally, this trick helps a slower centerboard boat win a race against a faster keel boat. It is usually necessary, though, that a very long leg of the race be with the wind astern. Many years ago at Casco Bay, Maine, I crewed on a centerboard boat that sailed by a much larger keel boat on the downwind leg to win the race. It was a victory I still cherish.

For reaching (see Glossary), the sail settings that lie between beating and running, the centerboard position is adjusted according to the position of the wind. The farther forward the wind, the lower the centerboard, until finally it is all the way down for beating.

As noted, the position of the centerboard can affect the helm. When a boat is perfectly balanced, the tiller (helm) should remain exactly in position when released, regardless of the point of sailing. Unfortunately, this is a condition that is very difficult to achieve. Usually there is either a *weather helm* or a *lee helm*. In a weather helm, the boat sails against the rudder and attempts to head up into the wind. The helmsman, consequently, must exert great force on the tiller to keep the boat on course. A lee helm is just the opposite; the boat turns away from the wind unless compensated for by the rudder. Sometimes a simple adjustment of the centerboard position will greatly improve a weather or lee helm. This is explained in Chapter 8.

A modern adaptation of the keel and centerboard combines the good characteristics of both. This is the combination keel-centerboard. In this type hull, usually seen on medium-size cruising-racing sailboats, the wineglass shape of a deep keel boat is cut off and a centerboard substituted for the bottom half of the keel. The keel-centerboard arrangement combines the stability of a keel boat with the shallow draft capability of a centerboarder. Many keel-centerboarders are in use today. They permit sailing under a wide range of weather and sea conditions, and also allow the skipper to take the boat very close to shore should he wish to.

Leeway, mentioned briefly earlier in the chapter, is the sideways motion of a sailboat resulting from the action of the wind and sea. When side pressure on a boat, such as when beating or reaching, is greatest, leeway is also at its greatest. In fact, running before the wind is the only point of sailing where there is no leeway.

The drawing shows the result of leeway. The top arrow shows the course steered. Notice how the boat points in this direction. Because of leeway, however, the boat actually sails along the path of the lower

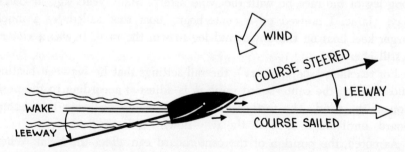

How leeway occurs. Wind side pressure on a boat makes it slip sideways at the same time that it is sailing forward. The angle of leeway is exaggerated in the drawing.

arrow. The angle between the two courses is the angle of leeway. As you can readily see, if you are planning a rather long sail, leeway has to be taken into account. More than once I've sailed across Long Island Sound only to find that leeway had brought me up far short of the point I wanted to reach. Many an inexperienced sailor has found himself sailing well into the night to make port because he neglected to take into account leeway, among other things.

You may see visual evidence of leeway if you look dead astern. This will appear as a very small angle between the wake and the line of the keel. As the drawing shows, this angle is also the angle of leeway.

No sailboat is immune to leeway. Whether daggerboard, centerboard, or keel, all boats make some leeway. Of course, as you may have guessed by now, the stronger the wind, that is, the greater the side pressure on the boat, the greater the leeway.

WOOD, FIBERGLASS, OR ALUMINUM?

Depending on the nature of the average wind and sea conditions under which the boat will be sailed, the object in buying a boat is to obtain a craft that will be fast, strong, seaworthy, and attractive to the eye. This can be done with any one of the major construction materials —wood, fiberglass, or aluminum. The choice is up to the buyer. It will help, though, to know something about the structural and performance characteristics of the different materials, as well as how hulls are put together. Of course, if you intend to race, you should look carefully at the types of boats being raced in your area.

Wood is the "granddaddy" of all boat construction materials. Its use dates back to the dawn of history, when men first fastened logs together and hollowed out felled tree trunks. The result of these thousands of years of experience with wood is that we know its properties quite well, and can build boats that will last for a great many years. Unlike fiberglass and aluminum, wood is relatively easy to work. Many repairs are well within the capability of the average man who is reasonably handy with woodworking tools. Decay and rot, which attack wood but not fiberglass and aluminum, are now relatively easy to control. Special wood preservatives that both prevent and stop rot are now available. They can be applied to an existing hull, or to the lumber going into a new hull at the time of construction.

Four different types of wood hulls are now in general use: the framed and planked hull with caulked seams; the flat- or V-bottom hull constructed of waterproof plywood sheets; the molded plywood hull, in which the plywood sheet is shaped over a hull form; and the strip-built hull, in which narrow strips are edge nailed and glued to each other over structural bulkheads.

Planked and caulked hulls are strong and flexible, yet they suffer from persistent and annoying leaks. Probably no other maintenance chore has gained the notoriety of caulking; most owners of wood boats are familiar with the feeling of discouragement that accompanies the tedious chore of caulking. Plywood planked hulls are strong and durable, yet they are not satisfactory to the skipper who desires an arc- or round-bottom hull. In addition, if they are not carefully constructed, the edges of the plywood planking may absorb water, resulting in separation of the laminated layers.

Molded plywood hulls, on the other hand, are extremely rigid and strong. These one-piece molded sheets are so strong that neither ribs nor frames are necessary. With waterproof glue eliminating many metal fastenings, the net result is a lightweight, easy-to-maintain hull. Strip-built hulls are supported by a few well-placed bulkheads rather than by ribs or frames. With the strips edge-nailed and cemented with waterproof glue, the net result is essentially a one-piece hull of very great strength. There are no seams to caulk, with the added advantage of a smooth interior.

When you go out to buy a sailboat, you will probably see far more *fiberglass* hulls than any other type. When such hulls are manufactured, the fiberglass is laid down on permanent molds, which are then used over and over again. The hull is usually molded in one piece; the topside, consisting of deck, cabin trunk, and cockpit, is also molded in one piece. The two parts are then fastened together. As you can see, the naval architect has great freedom when fiberglass is the hull material. It can be shaped in any manner desired. The next time you are near waters that serve the motorboat fraternity, take a closer look at some of the strange, radically different hull shapes. Speed-boat buffs, in particular, have a very wide choice of hull configurations.

Fiberglass as a construction material is still in its infancy. Experience with fiberglass dates back only to World War II. Indeed, it is said that the Navy is still using patrol boats molded during that war. Whatever the length of time it has been in use, however, fiberglass seems to be an exceptionally fine hull material if it is handled properly, with strict control of the manufacturing process.

Molded fiberglass is free from leaks, although fiberglass boats may leak at seams, around windows, and through fittings. All seats, berths, storage spaces, flotation materials, and other units can be molded in place. Some say fiberglass is unattractive because it lacks the warmth of wood. This is something you will have to decide for yourself when you buy, although more and more boat builders are including wood trim in the cockpits and cabins of their "glass" boats.

Despite the many good features that have led to wide use of fiberglass, it has some serious drawbacks. Probably most important, it has very little elasticity. There is no "give" when it is struck a hard blow. Thus one of two possibilities exists. Either the hull resists the blow or it fractures. In addition, fiberglass is very hard and dense. It is thus not easy to work with; repairs that might be easily made on a wood hull often stump the owner of a fiberglass boat. Finally, the slick, glossy surface of a "glass" boat is easily gouged and scraped by the objects it routinely comes into contact with during sailing. This surface, or *gelcoat*, is actually a thin layer of pigmented resin bonded to the hull. Its normal lifetime is about three years at the most. When refinishing is necessary, the whole hull must be painted, preferably with an epoxy-type marine paint.

Aluminum is just beginning to come into its own as a structural material for pleasure boats. It has been uphill all the way since the end of World War II, for right after that war aluminum boats acquired a very bad reputation. A great many boats were built using surplus aircraft aluminum, which unfortunately turned out to be incompatible with salt water. The boats corroded and came apart very quickly. Today's marine aluminum alloys, on the other hand, are extremely resistant to salt water corrosion. Boats built of these alloys have a very long corrosion-free lifetime.

In addition, greatly improved construction techniques now produce aluminum hulls of great structural strength. Along with the fact that they are considerably lighter in weight, aluminum hulls are less susceptible than wood and fiberglass to structural damage. Serious damage, however, can be a problem, for not many boatyards are equipped to repair aluminum hulls.

If you search, you will find a few small boats constructed of aluminum. Consider them carefully. Although they cost a little more to purchase, they more than repay this investment with liveliness under sail, a high resale value, and simpler maintenance.

3. Nautical Terminology

Before we go any further, it is necessary that you become familiar with the most important nautical terms related to sailing. As we progress into the details of sailing theory and sailboat operation, these terms will be used repeatedly. Thus, to follow the text with understanding, you should become familiar with the glossary that follows, and then refer to it whenever you are in doubt about the meaning of a word.

Your first task is to learn the names and functions of the major parts of a sailboat. Although this is no easy chore for someone who has little or no experience with sailing, it is necessary if you are to master the sailing skills needed to get you out on the water. Refer to the diagram. These are the most important parts of a sailboat. All of these terms are included in the glossary. Look them up now one by one, and try to remember the description and purpose of each one.

A very good way to make sailboat rigging and terms come alive before actually going aboard a boat is to build a scale model. Choose a sloop, since this is the type of boat you are most likely to sail on. These models are available in hobby shops, in either wood or preformed plastic. Follow the assembly instructions carefully, keeping in mind that what you are working on in miniature has its direct counterpart on a real sailboat. After completing the model, set up a small fan and produce the wind conditions discussed in Chapter 8. You will find this a useful aid in understanding the wind forces on a boat.

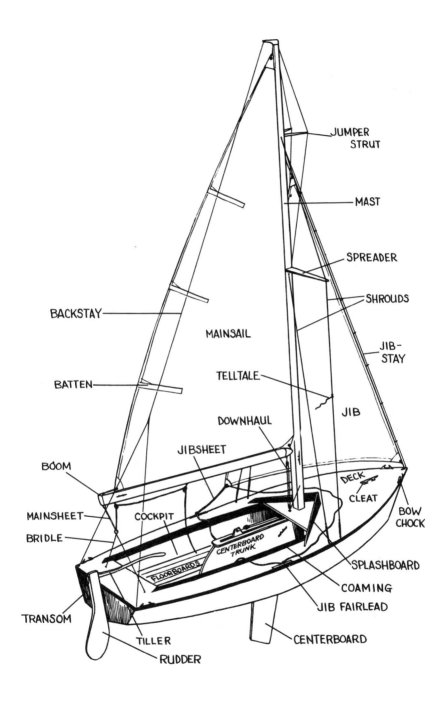

JUMPER STRUT

MAST

SPREADER

SHROUDS

JIB-STAY

JUMPER STRUT

BACKSTAY

MAINSAIL

TELLTALE

JIB

BATTEN

DOWNHAUL

JIBSHEET

BOOM

DECK

CLEAT

BOW CHOCK

MAINSHEET

COCKPIT

BRIDLE

CENTERBOARD TRUNK

FLOORBOARDS

SPLASHBOARD

COAMING

JIB FAIRLEAD

TRANSOM

TILLER

RUDDER

CENTERBOARD

GLOSSARY

ABAFT: further aft; "abaft the beam," for example, is aft of the beam.

ABEAM: off the side of a boat at an angle of 90 degrees to the fore-and-aft centerline.

AFT: in the direction of the stern.

AHEAD: in the direction of the vessel's bow.

ALEE: away from the direction of the wind.

AMIDSHIPS: at the center of a vessel, in terms of either length or width.

ANCHOR: an iron or steel device designed to hold a vessel when dropped to the bottom.

ANCHORAGE: a suitable place for dropping anchor.

ASTERN: in the direction of the vessel's stern.

BACKSTAY: a wire-rope mast support leading aft from the top of a mast to the deck or to another mast.

BACKWIND: a wind that strikes the leeward (away from the wind) side of a sail after it has passed over another sail.

BALLAST: heavy weight placed at or near the bottom of a sailboat to provide stability.

BALLOON JIB: a large jib with a draft deeper than that of a genoa jib; used for reaching in light winds.

BARE POLES: no sails set, as in "running under bare poles" in a gale.

BAROMETER: an instrument that measures atmospheric pressure.

BATTENS: thin, rigid strips that fit into pockets along the after edge of a sail; battens help to hold the shape of a sail.

BEAM: the greatest width of a vessel, usually amidships.

BEAM WIND: a wind blowing at right angles to the fore-and-aft centerline of a vessel.

BEARING: the direction of an object from a vessel relative to the vessel's heading, or by compass.

BEAT: to sail to windward by alternate tacks.

BEFORE THE WIND: sailing with the wind astern, that is, with the wind coming from directly behind the vessel; see *running*.

BEND: to fasten a sail to the boom and mast; also to fasten one rope to another.

BILGE: the portion of the inside hull below the floorboards.

BOOM: spar at the bottom of a mainsail or mizzensail on sloops, yawls, and ketches, and other sailing vessels.

BOOM CRUTCH: a support that holds the boom off the deck when it is not in use.

BOOM VANG: a rig attached to the boom to hold it down and thus to flatten the sail.

BOW: the forward part of the hull of a vessel.

BOW CHOCKS: metal fittings situated on either side of the bow that lead anchor or mooring lines inboard.

BOWLINE: a knot used to form a loop at the end of a line.

BREAKWATER: a sea wall that breaks the force of waves.

BRIDLE: a span of rope to which the mainsheet, and sometimes the spinnaker pole, is attached.

BRIGHTWORK: varnished woodwork and polished brass aboard a vessel.

BRISTOL FASHION: in a seamanlike manner.

BROACH: to swing around toward the wind when running free, thus placing the vessel broadside to wind and waves.

BROAD REACH: a sailing course between beam reaching and running before the wind, with the wind coming from of the quarter.

BUOY: a floating marker used for piloting; see *can buoy* and *nun buoy*.

BURDENED VESSEL: a vessel required by law to stay clear of another vessel holding the right of way.

BY THE LEE: running with the wind on the same side as the boom.

CAN BUOY: a black cylindrical buoy carrying an odd number that marks the left, or port side of a channel when a vessel is approaching from seaward.

CAPSIZE: to overturn.

CAST OFF: to release a line; in general, to let go all lines and leave a dock.

CATAMARAN: a twin-hulled vessel.

CAT BOAT: a sailboat having one mast set well forward and no headsails.

CENTERBOARD: a hinged plate housed in a trunk or well along the centerline of a sailboat, and lowered below the bottom of the hull to reduce leeway when sailing to windward.

CENTERBOARD TRUNK: the housing for a centerboard when it is not lowered into place.

CHAIN PLATES: metal straps bolted to the side of a vessel that secure the shrouds.

CHART: a nautical map.

CHINE: intersection of a hull's side and bottom.

CHOCK: a metal fitting that leads lines over the side of a vessel.

CLEAT: a horn-shaped fitting used to secure a line.

CLEW: the aftermost corner of a fore-and-aft-rigged sail.

CLOSEHAULED: sailing as close to the direction of the wind as efficiency permits.

CLOSE REACH: a sailing course between beating and beam reaching, with the wind forward of the beam.

CLOVE HITCH: two half hitches thrown around a spar or another rope.

COAMING: raised railing around a cockpit to prevent water from running in.

COCKPIT: opening at after end of a sailboat for passengers or feet.

COIL: to lay a rope in a circular pattern.

COME UP INTO THE WIND: steer the vessel toward the eye of the wind; see *head up* and *luff up*.

COMING ABOUT: going from one tack to the other by passing the bow through the eye of the wind.

COMPASS COURSE: a vessel's heading based on the vessel's compass.

COMPASS ROSE: a graduated circle carrying the points of the compass and printed on a chart.

COURSE: the heading of a vessel as measured by the compass.

CRINGLE: ring sewn into a sail through which a line can be passed.

CUDDY: a small shelter cabin forward of the cockpit on many sailboats.

CURRENT: the horizontal movement of water caused by tide, wind, or gravity.

DAGGERBOARD: a type of centerboard not hinged, but rather raised and lowered vertically in the trunk.

DECK: the floor or horizontal surface of a vessel.

DINGHY (DINK):   a small open boat.

DISPLACEMENT: the weight of water displaced by a vessel, thus the vessel's own weight.

DOUSE: to lower or drop suddenly, as in "douse the sails."

DOWNHAUL: a line used to pull down the tack of a sail.

DRAFT: the "belly" or fullness of a sail; also the depth of water needed to float a vessel.

EBB TIDE: the tide during its passage from high to low water.

EVEN KEEL: floating level, not heeled over or listing.

EYE OF THE WIND: the exact direction from which the wind is coming.

EYE SPLICE: a loop spliced in the end of a rope.

FAIRLEAD: a fitting that changes the direction of a rope lead.

FATHOM: a unit of measure equal to six feet.

FENDER: a cushion that prevents a boat's side from striking a dock or the side of another boat.

FIGURE EIGHT KNOT: a knot tied in the end of a line to prevent it from running through a block.

FISHERMAN'S BEND: a method for making the anchor line fast to the anchor.

FLOOD TIDE: the tide during its passage from low to high water.

FLOORBOARDS: planking on the bottom of the cockpit.

FLOTSAM: floating debris.

FOGBOUND: held in port or at anchor because of fog.

FORE-AND-AFT: in line or parallel with the keel.

FORWARD: in front of, as in "forward of the beam."

FOUL: snarl or tangle; the opposite of clear.

FOUND: furnished; a vessel is said to be "well found" if it is well equipped.

FREEBOARD: the distance from the top of the hull to the water.

FULL AND BY: all sails full and drawing on a course as close to the wind as
   possible.

GAFF: a spar that supports the head of a fore-and-aft-rigged sail; as in "gaff-
   rigged" and "gaff-headed."

GENOA: a large jib whose area overlaps the mainsail.

SCHOONER YACHT *America*

The new schooner *America* was launched in 1967, 116 years to the
day after her famous ancestor was launched in New York. The original
America started the America's Cup tradition in 1851 by defeating seventeen British yachts. At that time the *Illustrated London News* referred
to her as a "rakish, piratical-looking craft." Built to honor "those seafaring
traditions and spirit which contributed so importantly to the greatness
of our land," the new *America* was reproduced from the original *America's* lines. Faithfully reproduced throughout her exterior, the yacht is
completely modern below decks. She boasts air conditioning, luxury
cruising accommodations, and a powerful diesel engine. No type of
sailing vessel is more American than the schooner, as the *America* clearly
demonstrates. (Photo by Peter Barlow)

GHOSTING: making headway when there is no apparent wind.

GOOSENECK: the fitting that fastens the boom to the mast.

GROUND SWELL: long waves coming from seaward.

GROUND TACKLE: a term used to cover all anchor and mooring gear.

GUDGEON: an eye fitting on the transom into which the rudder's *pintle* is inserted.

GUNWALE: the rail of a vessel at deck level.

HALF HITCH: a turn around a spar or rope with the end coming through the bight (the bight is the portion of the rope between the ends).

HALYARDS: lines used to hoist the sails.

HARD-A-LEE: the final command in the tacking or coming-about sequence; it is given just before putting the tiller over hard to the side opposite the wind.

HAUL: to pull on a line; also said of wind that has shifted toward the bow.

HEADSAILS: all sails set forward of the foremast (the single mast on a sloop).

HEADSTAY: a wire-rope mast support running from the top or near the top of the mast to the bow.

HEAD UP: to point the bow of the vessel more nearly into the wind; see *luff up.*

HEADWAY: motion ahead.

HEAVE: to throw, as in "heave a line"; also the rise and fall of a vessel in a seaway.

HEEL: to tip or list to one side.

HELM: the tiller or wheel.

HIKE: to climb to windward on a sailboat to prevent excessive heeling to leeward.

HITCH: a method of making a rope fast to another object.

HULL: the body of a vessel, not including spars and gear.

IN IRONS: the condition of a sailboat, head to wind with the sails luffing, with the bow not paying off on either tack; also called *in stays.*

INSHORE: toward the shore.

JETSAM: articles that sink when thrown overboard.

JETTISON: to throw overboard.

JIB: a triangular sail set forward of the foremast (the single mast on a sloop).

JIBE: to change a sailboat's course from one tack to the other with the wind aft.

JIB FAIRLEAD: an eye or fitting that conducts the jibsheet into the cockpit.

JIB-HEADED: a tall rig with a triangular mainsail.

JIBSHEET: the line from the lower aft end of the jib to the cockpit; used to control the set of the jib.

JIBSTAY: the forward stay, or forestay, to which the leading edge of the jib is attached.

JUMPER STRUT: a strut placed aloft on the forward side of the mast for added support.

JURY RIG: any makeshift rig.

KEDGE: a small anchor used for warping (pulling) a vessel forward.

KEDGING OUT: to free a vessel aground or move away from a lee dock by hauling on a kedge anchor.

KEEL: the fore-and-aft timber along the centerline of a vessel; on keel sailboats, the keel extends well below the rest of the hull and provides weight stability and lateral resistance.

KETCH: a two-masted sailboat having the aftermast forward of the rudder post.

KNOCKABOUT: the correct (although rarely used) term for a sloop without a bowsprit.

KNOCKDOWN: when a vessel is thrown on its beam ends by a sudden gust of wind.

KNOT: a measure of speed meaning *nautical miles per hour* (one nautical mile equals 6o8o.2o feet); also a method of binding objects together using rope.

LAND BREEZE: an evening breeze blowing from land to sea.

LANDLUBBER: sailor's term for a person unfamiliar with the sea and seafaring.

LAZARETTE: below deck storage space aft.

LEECH: the trailing edge of a fore-and-aft sail.

LEE HELM: an unbalanced condition that tends to turn the sailboat away from the wind; the opposite of *weather helm*, which is more desirable.

LEEWARD: away from the direction of the wind.

LEEWAY: the distance a sailboat is carried to leeward by the force of the wind.

LINES: ropes on a vessel that are used for special purposes, such as *sheet lines, bow lines,* or *guy lines.*

LOOSE-FOOTED: a sail fastened to a boom at tack and clew only, or without a boom.

LUFF: the forward edge of a sail; also the fluttering of a sail as it begins to be backwinded.

LUFF UP: to steer more closely into the wind; see *head up.*

MAGNETIC BEARING: the direction of an object from the heading of a vessel, with no deviation.

MAGNETIC COURSE: the heading of a vessel based on the magnetic compass.

MAINSAIL: fore-and-aft sail set on the after side of the mainmast.

MAINSHEET: the line from the main boom to the cockpit; used to control the set of the mainsail.

MARCONI: tall jib-headed triangular sails.

MARLINSPIKE: a pointed tool used for separating rope or wire strands when splicing.

MAST: a vertical spar that supports spars, rigging, and sails.

MASTHEAD: the top of the mast; a rig in which the headsails extend to the top of the mast.

MIZZENMAST: the after and shorter of the two masts on yawls and ketches.

MOORING: a large permanent anchor and buoy; generally a vessel's permanent home.

NAUTICAL MILE: a unit of distance equal to 6080.20 feet; see *knot.*

NUN BUOY: a conical red buoy carrying an even number and marking the right, or starboard side of a channel entering from seaward.

OFFSHORE: away from the shore.

OFF THE WIND: sailing on any course except to windward.

ON THE WIND: sailing to windward; see *beat* and *closehauled.*

OUTBOARD: beyond the side of a vessel.

OUTHAUL: a line used to fasten and tighten the clew of a sail.

PAINTER: a short length of rope attached to the bow of a small boat.

PAY OFF: to swing away from the wind.

PAY OUT: to ease or feed out a rope.

PENNANT: a small narrow flag; also the length of rope that attaches a vessel to its mooring float.

PINCHING: sailing too close to the wind.

PINTLE: a pinlike metal fitting on the rudder that inserts into the *gudgeon*, which is attached to the boat's transom.

POINT: the ability to sail to windward; a sailboat that "points well" sails close to the wind.

PORT: the left side of a vessel facing forward.

PORT TACK: sailing with the wind coming in to the boat over the port side.

PRAM: a small dinghy having square ends.

PRIVILEGED VESSEL: the vessel holding the right of way; the *burdened vessel* must keep clear.

QUARTER: that portion of a vessel forward of the stern and aft of the beam.

QUARTERING SEA: a sea running toward either the port or starboard quarter of a vessel.

RAIL: the outer edge of the deck on a vessel.

RAKE: the angle of a mast from the vertical.

REACH: a sailing course between running free and closehauled.

READY ABOUT: the initial order given when it is desired to bring a sailboat about.

REEF: a technique for reducing sail area.

REEF POINTS: short pieces of line attached to a sail and used to tie in a reef.

RIG: the nature of a sailboat's mast and sail arrangement, as in cat rig, jib-headed rig, and gaff rig.

RIGGING: a term applying to all lines, stays, and shrouds on a sailboat.

RIGHT: to return a vessel to its normal position, as in "righting a capsized boat."

RIGHT OF WAY: the right of the privileged vessel to hold course and speed.

ROACH: the curve along the leech of a sail.

RODE: the anchor line or cable.

RUDDER: the flat plate hinged at or near the stern that is used to steer a vessel; the rudder is controlled by the *tiller.*

RULES OF THE ROAD: the laws of navigation; their primary purpose is the avoidance of collisions.

RUNNING: sailing on a course with the wind astern or on the quarter; see *before the wind.*

RUNNING RIGGING: the movable part of a sailboat's rigging; for example, the halyards and sheet lines.

SCOPE: the length of anchor line let out.

SEA ANCHOR: a dragging device used to slow a vessel down in heavy weather.

SEAWAY: an area of sea with moderate or heavy seas running.

SEAWORTHY: capable of putting to sea and meeting sea conditions.

SHEET: a line that controls the set of the sails; see *jibsheet* and *mainsheet.*

SHIPSHAPE: neat and seamanlike.

SHOOT UP INTO THE WIND: to steer the sailboat's bow into the eye of the wind under the boat's momentum.

SHOVE OFF: to depart.

SHROUDS: the rigging that supports a mast at its sides.

SLACK: to ease off; also loose or unfastened; also the state of the tide when there is no horizontal water motion.

SLOOP: a one-masted sailboat, carrying mainsail and jib.

SNUB: to check or stop a rope suddenly.

SPAR: a term applied to masts, booms, gaffs, etc.

SPINNAKER: a light balloonlike sail used when running and reaching.

SPLASHBOARD: a raised board on deck designed to deflect spray away from the cockpit.

SPLICE: a method for weaving strands of rope together.

SPREADER: a horizontal strut to which shrouds are attached to support the mast.

THE BARK *Eagle*

One of the few remaining square-riggers in use, the U. S. Coast Guard Academy's bark *Eagle* was built in Germany in 1936. The Academy uses the vessel as a training ship. Each year during the month of June cadets of the first and third classes board the *Eagle* and depart on a two-and-a-half-month cruise to Europe or the Caribbean. For many of the cadets, this cruise is the fulfillment of a lifelong dream. The young cadets stand watches and perform all the duties that enlisted men carry out aboard the average Coast Guard cutter. They become familiar with every detail of the *Eagle,* on deck and aloft. In addition to learning seamanship under the most demanding of conditions, the cadets develop leadership and initiative. Not many young sailors have the good fortune to ship out on a vessel such as the *Eagle.* (Photo by U. S. Coast Guard Academy)

SPRING LINE: a dock line leading forward or aft that keeps a vessel from moving ahead or astern.

SQUALL: a sudden and violent local storm or gust of wind.

SQUARE KNOT: a knot consisting of two overhand knots.

STANDING RIGGING: the part of a sailboat's rigging, that is, the *shrouds* and *stays*, that support the mast.

STARBOARD: the right side of a vessel facing forward.

STARBOARD TACK: sailing with the wind coming in to the boat over the starboard side.

STAYS: the rigging running forward and aft that supports the mast; see *backstay, headstay,* and *jibstay.*

STAYSAIL: a fore-and-aft triangular sail normally set on a stay; sometimes staysails are set flying.

STEERAGE WAY: sufficient headway for the rudder to function.

STERN: the after end of a vessel.

STORM JIB: a small triangular sail used in very heavy weather.

STOW: to store away on a vessel.

SWAMP: to sink by filling with water.

TACK: to come about; also the lower forward corner of a sail; also a course sailed, such as the *port tack* and the *starboard tack.*

TACKLE: a combination of blocks and rope—a "block and tackle."

TAUT: having no slack.

TELLTALE: a strip of ribbon or yarn tied to a shroud to show the direction of the apparent wind.

TENDER: lacking stability; also a small boat used for ferrying passengers.

THWARTSHIPS: at right angles to the fore-and-aft line on a vessel; from side to side.

TIDE: the rise and fall of the sea level.

TIDE RIPS: areas of disturbed and turbulent water caused by strong tidal currents.

TILLER: a rod used to control the rudder.

TOPPING LIFT: a rope used to support a boom from above.

TOPSIDE: on deck.

TOPSIDES: the sides of a vessel between the waterline and the rail.

TRANSOM: the stern planking of a square-sterned vessel.

TRAVELER: a metal rod that allows a sheet block to slide back and forth; if rope is used instead, it becomes a *bridle*.

TRIM: the fore-and-aft balance of a vessel; also to adjust the sails to take best advantage of the wind.

TRUE COURSE: a course that has been corrected for variation and deviation.

TURNBUCKLE: a thread-and-screw device used to adjust the tension in shrouds and stays.

UNDER WAY: in motion and under control of the helmsman.

UP ANCHOR: the command to raise the anchor and get under way.

VANG: see *boom vang*.

VARIATION: the local differences in degrees between true north and magnetic north.

VEER: when the wind changes direction toward the stern.

WAKE: the track a vessel leaves astern as it passes through the water.

WATERLINE: a line painted on a vessel's side to indicate its proper trim.

WEATHER HELM: an unbalanced condition that tends to turn the sailboat toward the wind; the opposite of *lee helm*.

WEATHER SIDE: the windward side.

WELL FOUND: a well-equipped vessel with all gear in good condition.

WHIPPING: twine or thread wound around the end of a rope to keep it from fraying.

WHISKER POLE: a spar used to hold the clew of the jib away from the boat when running before the wind.

WINDWARD: toward the wind; the weather side of a vessel.

WINCH: a mechanical device used to haul sheet lines.

WING-AND-WING: running before the wind with the main and jib set on opposite sides of the boat.

WORKING SAILS: mainsail and jib used for ordinary weather conditions.

YACHT: any vessel designed for pleasure use.

YAW: to steer uncontrollably out of the line of the course, as when running with a heavy quartering sea.

YAWL: a two-masted sailboat having the aftermast abaft the rudder post.

4. What Makes a Sailboat Go?

To the uninformed observer, one of the most astonishing things about fore-and-aft-rigged sailboats is that many of them can be sailed to 45 degrees or closer to the direction of the wind. Despite the apparent pushing effect of the wind in the opposite direction, the boat moves diagonally into the wind. On the other hand, it's easy to see why a floating box, a cork, or a sailboat moves along with the wind behind it; in a very real way the object is being pushed along by the wind. These are the two sailing extremes; *running*, with the wind dead astern, and *beating to windward*, with the wind 45 degrees or more ahead. In general, the same explanation applies to both extremes. Unfortunately, this explanation is a bit complicated, and involves some simple principles of aerodynamics. To grasp fully, however, why sailboats behave as they do, and to prepare yourself properly to handle a sailboat, you should understand this aerodynamic explanation. With it safely tucked away in your mind, you will never again scratch your head in wonderment at the seemingly strange behavior of sailboats.

THE SAIL AS AN AIRFOIL

While other parts of a sailboat, such as the hull, keel, and rudder no doubt help it to move, the action of the wind on the sails is the major source of driving power. It is how this drive is generated by the sails that interests us. Sails, as you will see later, are cut and sewn so that they are curved, much in the same way an airplane wing is curved. There is a good reason for this.

Let's look at how an airplane wing resembles a sail. As the drawing shows, an airplane wing is curved on top and relatively straight along the bottom. Now, when a stream of air passes over the wing, the stream divides; part goes under the wing and part goes above it. But the air going above the wing must travel a greater distance along the curve than the air passing over the flat surface along the bottom. It turns out that the air streaming over the top moves *faster* than the air moving across the bottom of the wing. This is easy to see; since the top air must go a greater distance in the same time, it must go faster. This is where the upward force on a wing, or *lift*, comes in. As the speed of airflow increases, the pressure it exerts decreases. Thus the pressure of the air on top of the wing is less than the pressure of the air on the bottom. The difference in pressure is the lift.

You can prove this point for yourself. Take a sheet of notebook paper, and as the drawing suggests, blow vigorously slightly down and across the top surface. The movement of your breath across the top is much faster than the movement of air underneath. What happens to the paper? Do you see how the difference in pressure creates lift on the piece of paper?

Much the same thing happens on sails when the wind is on the beam

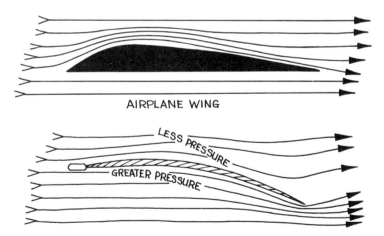

AIRPLANE WING

The airplane wing is a high-speed airfoil, while the sail is a low-speed airfoil. In both cases, however, lift or drive is generated because there is less pressure on the convex side of the airfoil.

44

or forward of the beam. As the wind strikes the sail and divides, the difference in wind speed across the two surfaces creates a difference in pressure. This difference is the *driving force* of the sail. It occurs in the *luff*, the forward third of the sail, and is the equivalent of lift in an airplane wing. But because of the way a sail is mounted, this driving force is directed more toward the bow than toward the side of the boat.

Experiments with sails in wind tunnels show the effectiveness of this driving force on different points of sailing. When a boat is sailing close-hauled, about 75 percent of the total drive comes from the pressure differential force. When a boat is running, however, with the wind dead astern, only about 25 percent of the total drive is the pressure differential force. The remaining 75 percent is the result of direct wind pressure on the sail. Thus, in a manner of speaking, a boat beating to windward

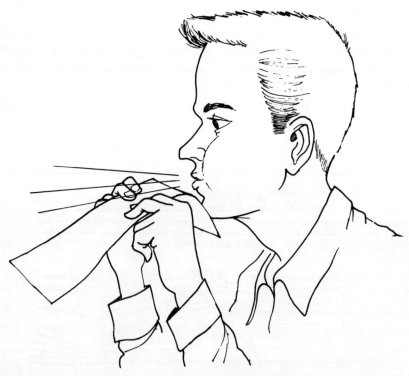

See for yourself that pressure decreases as the speed of airflow increases. Blow slightly downward and across the top of the paper. Why does the paper rise?

is primarily pulled forward by the lift generated as the wind passes over the sails, while a boat running before the wind is primarily pushed forward by the positive pressure of the wind coming from behind the boat.

THE SLOT EFFECT

As you have probably guessed by now, the faster the wind travels over the convex side of a sail the greater the drive generated. But there is a way to get even more drive. This is where the jib comes in. The jib does two things when a boat is sailing to windward or reaching. It is an airfoil in its own right, and generates drive. But even more important, it funnels air between itself and the convex side of the mainsail. When a stream of air is compressed into a smaller volume, as between the jib and main, the air's speed increases, although there may be turbulence. If the jib is trimmed properly, however, its effect greatly increases the speed and smoothness of flow of the air passing between the sails. As a result, the drive generated by the mainsail is considerably increased. This is the *slot effect*. The drawing shows what happens to the airstream when the jib is eased off too far or trimmed too flat, and finally, how the airstream behaves when the jib is set just right. Clearly, this is the most important function served by the jib. In addition, the farther aft the jib extends behind the mainsail the greater the slot effect. This is the principal reason for the larger jibs, called *genoa jibs,* that you see so frequently. By extending farther aft they form a deeper slot, thus further funneling the airstream and creating even greater drive.

WIND FORCES ON A SAILBOAT

As mentioned, the wind generates a driving force forward as it comes into contact with and passes over the sails. But with the exception of running, with the wind dead astern, a portion of the wind's energy works to make the boat heel and make leeway. Put another way, the wind does two things: It drives the boat forward, and it exerts a sideways force on the boat. Just how the wind acts to produce heeling, leeway, and forward drive is not generally well understood. To be a better sailor, however, you should know something about these effects.

Let's use simple force diagrams to describe how the wind's energy

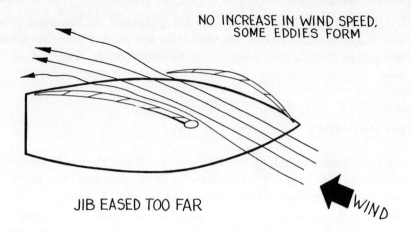

NO INCREASE IN WIND SPEED,
SOME EDDIES FORM

WIND

JIB EASED TOO FAR

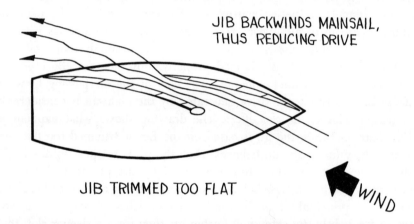

JIB BACKWINDS MAINSAIL,
THUS REDUCING DRIVE

WIND

JIB TRIMMED TOO FLAT

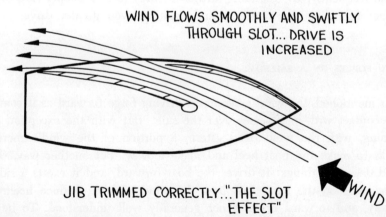

WIND FLOWS SMOOTHLY AND SWIFTLY
THROUGH SLOT... DRIVE IS
INCREASED

WIND

JIB TRIMMED CORRECTLY..."THE SLOT
EFFECT"

"The slot effect." When the jib is trimmed correctly, the passage of air through the "slot" is speeded up. Greater drive is the result.

"The slot effect" is very evident in this shot of a Viking 140 on Long Island Sound. Note how the shape of the jib funnels and speeds up the air passing between the sails. This effect greatly increases the drive of the mainsail. (Photo by James Pazzi, courtesy of Viking of America)

is divided on different points of sailing. To keep the explanation as simple as possible, we will avoid unnecessary details, but yet include the most important aspects of the problem. To begin with, we will let arrows represent the wind forces. As the diagram shows, these forces are: F, the total wind force; S, the sideways force that produces heel and leeway; and D, the thrust that drives the boat forward.

At this point, if you have looked at the drawings carefully, you undoubtedly have a question. Why does the arrow F indicate that the total wind energy acts on the mast, if the driving force is generated in the forward third, the luff, of the mainsail? In somewhat simplified form, the answer is that both mainsail and jib do indeed generate drive in the forward third of the sail, but they in turn act on the mast to push the boat along. We are simplifying by assuming that all of the thrust is concentrated on the mast. Another question that may have occurred to you is this: Why are the arrows drawn with their tails to the mast, rather than the other way around? It is done this way simply for the sake of convenience. After all, does it really matter if the diagram is behind the mast and on the other side of the outline of the hull, or where we have drawn it?

Now let's look at the force diagrams, starting with the boat that is closehauled. The total wind force developed by the sail is F; notice its direction. This total force does two things. It drives the boat forward with that portion of the total force equal to force of D. But another portion of the total force equal to S pushes the boat sideways. The diagram is drawn as a right triangle because two forces, S and D, acting together at right angles to each other produce the same result as the single force F.

Now look at the boat sailing on a beam reach, that is, with the wind at right angles to the course of the boat. Sailing with the wind in this position, the sails are not sheeted in as tightly. As a result, the total force F points more toward the bow of the boat. On a broad reach, the sails are trimmed even farther out, and the total force F points even closer to the bow. Finally, when the wind is dead astern, virtually all of the force is directly ahead.

The important point to note in these diagrams is that the drive portion D of the total wind force F is smallest when the boat is closehauled, and that it increases as the boat's course is changed in the direction of reaching. As you can see, because the sideways force S is largest when the boat is closehauled, this is the point of sailing that will produce the greatest heeling and the greatest leeway. But the centerboard or keel,

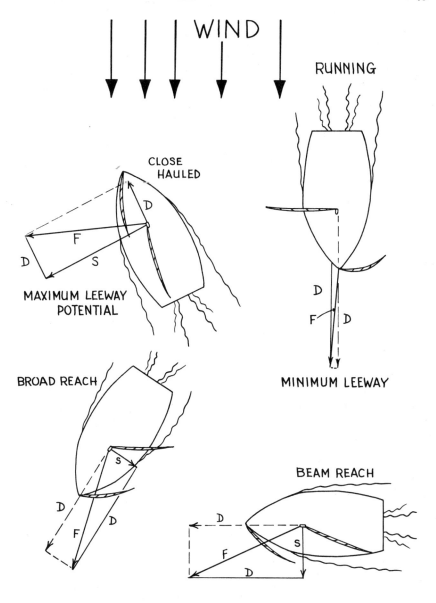

F = TOTAL WIND FORCE
S = SIDEWAYS FORCE (HEEL AND LEEWAY)
D = FORWARD DRIVE THRUST

Force diagrams show the relationship between total wind force, sideways force, and forward drive thrust.

you will recall, offers lateral resistance to movement of the boat, thus reducing leeway. Heeling occurs because the boat resists sideways motion; it rotates on an axis that runs the length of the boat near the waterline. But as the boat heels, air spills out of the sails. Finally, the boat stops heeling when the forces on the hull tending to right it just equalize the wind pressure tending to heel the boat over.

Since a great deal of sailing is done with the boat heeled over, it is important to know how much of the sail is exposed to the wind for various angles of heel. As the drawing shows, less and less sail is exposed to the wind as the angle of heel increases. In part, this is a safety valve, for when there is less sail exposed, a greater amount of wind spills out of the sails. By the same token, however, the smaller the sail area

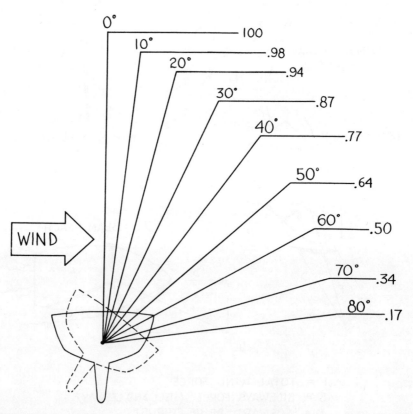

The amount of sail exposed to the wind at various angles of heel. For example, at fifty degrees of heel only 64 percent of the sail is exposed to the wind.

exposed to the wind the smaller the driving thrust generated. In strong, gusty winds the skipper must be very alert. Centerboard boats, in particular, may be knocked down or capsized, sometimes catching the skipper and crew completely by surprise.

FUNCTION OF THE TILLER

In a small sailboat, the skipper usually has both hands fully occupied. In one hand he controls the mainsheet, the line that sets the position of the mainsail, and with the other he operates the tiller. The tiller is a handle fitted to the head of the rudder post. It extends forward into the cockpit, placing it in a convenient position for handling.

Moving the tiller moves the rudder, and thus controls the direction of sailing. As the drawing shows, when the tiller is moved to port (left, facing forward) the stern moves to port and the bow turns to starboard (right, facing forward). Conversely, when the tiller is moved to starboard, the stern moves to starboard and the bow turns to port. When the tiller and rudder are in line with the keel, of course, there is no turning effect.

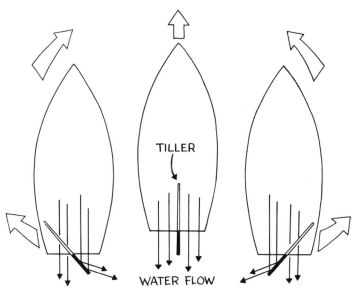

Water forces on the rudder, and how a boat turns. Note that in a turn the stern shifts to the side to point the boat in the new direction.

It is sometimes hard for beginners to grasp just how a boat turns. Many believe that boats turn the same way autos do, that is, the front end turns and the rear end follows the path the front end describes. This is not the case at all with boats. On a car, the steering is accomplished by wheels that turn at the front. On a boat, the rudder is mounted at the stern. Thus, one literally points the front of a car in the direction desired, while on a boat the position of the stern is shifted until the bow points in the desired direction. Many an inexperienced sailor has been embarrassed by ramming neighboring boats or a dock with a swinging stern. As you will see later, maneuvering a boat in tight situations presents altogether different problems from those met in an automobile.

Look at the drawing again. It shows how inserting the rudder into the smooth stream of water passing under the boat makes the boat change course. As the rudder is turned, it interferes with the passage of flowing water. The water thus exerts pressure on the side of the rudder facing forward. This pressure causes the stern to swing in the direction the tiller is pointing. Of course, when the rudder is in line with the keel, the water pressure on both sides is the same, and no turning effect occurs.

There are two additional points worth noting. First, because a turned rudder interferes with the flow of water around the hull, it has a braking effect on the speed of a boat. Second, there is a rudder angle for every boat that produces the greatest turning effect. If the rudder is turned to a greater angle, its effect is to slow the boat down more than to turn it. In the extreme, if the rudder is turned a full 90 degrees, it does little or no turning and acts mostly as a brake.

As you have probably noticed, for the rudder to exert a turning effect water must be flowing around it. But, of course, for water to stream by the rudder, the boat must be under way. That is, it must be moving. In nautical terms, *steerage way* is the slowest speed at which a boat can be steered. At lower speeds the boat simply does not respond to the helm; in a sense, it is nearly dead in the water.

Sailboats should be easy to steer. Indeed, if a boat is well balanced, the tiller is quite light to the touch. One hand is usually sufficient; sometimes it is even possible to handle the tiller with just the fingertips. It is important to remember that rudder movements should be smooth and gentle, with the smallest possible movement. Sharply yanking the tiller back and forth slows a boat, for as pointed out, a turned rudder exerts a braking effect.

One of the funniest episodes I have ever seen on the water involved a tiller. A friend, a burly, swarthy six-footer, was out sailing one day with his wife when he found himself in an impromptu race with another boat of the same class. The two boats—twenty-four-foot cruising sloops —were sailing to windward about fifteen yards apart when suddenly the tiller on my friend's boat broke off at the head of the rudder. The boat immediately turned sharply into the wind, heading straight for the other boat. A collision seemed inevitable. Surprised, and somewhat frightened, my friend immediately leaped to the bow of his boat and waved the broken tiller in the air toward the other boat. He wanted to warn the other skipper that his tiller had broken. Unfortunately, all the other poor man could see was a sailboat bearing down on him at full speed with a huge man at the bow waving what looked like a club. You can imagine his reaction. The day was saved by my friend's wife. She had the good sense to release the jib and mainsheet lines, thus loosing the sails. The boat stopped dead in the water just a few yards from the other one. A very unusual accident, to be sure, but one that demonstrates that the good sailor must be ready for any unexpected change.

THE BEAUFORT WIND SCALE

At this time, while the idea of wind force and how a sailboat reacts to the wind are fresh in your mind, it seems a good idea to introduce the wind force scale. Clearly, it is important that you know how winds of different strengths affect the sea. No doubt you have heard such terms as "moderate breeze," "whole gale," and "hurricane." Up until now these terms probably meant little to you, aside from the fact that they conveyed a general idea of what the weather was like. As a sailor, however, you will need to know much more about them, for you will make many decisions based on wind force and sea conditions. For example, do you go out or stay in port? Do you use a storm jib, working jib, or genoa jib? Should you reef the mainsail, or isn't it necessary? Should everybody on board be wearing life jackets? And so on. Sea conditions are the result of wind action. Good sailors know the relationship between the two, and make correct decisions on the basis of this knowledge. Read the table carefully. It may help you avoid a dunking (at the least), or a mishap of major proportions (at the most).

TABLE I—BEAUFORT WIND SCALE

Code Figure	Beaufort's Scale	Effect on Sea	Velocity (Knots)
0	Calm	Sea smooth, mirrorlike.	Less than 1
1	Light air	Some ripples, no foamy tops.	1-3
2	Light breeze	Small wavelets, tops appear glassy but do not break.	4-6
3	Gentle breeze	Large wavelets. Occasional whitecaps.	7-10
4	Moderate breeze	Small waves increasing in length. Frequent whitecaps.	11-16
5	Fresh breeze	Moderate waves further increasing in length. Many whitecaps with spray.	17-21
6	Strong breeze	Large waves beginning to appear. Whitecaps everywhere, much spray.	22-27
7	Moderate gale	Large breaking waves. Foam begins to be blown in streaks in direction of wind.	28-33

TABLE I—BEAUFORT WIND SCALE (cont'd)

8	Fresh gale	Moderately high waves. Tops break off and are blown in direction of wind.	34-40
9	Strong gale	High waves. Heavy foam streaks blown by wind. Sea beginning to roll, and spray may interfere with visibility.	41-47
10	Whole gale	Very high waves. Sea appears white all over. Heavy rolling of seas. Visibility seriously affected.	48-55
11	Storm	Extremely high waves. Medium-sized ships become lost to view for long periods of time.	56-63
12-17	Hurricane	Air filled with foam and spray. Waves higher than forty-five feet. Sea completely white with driving spray. Visibility extremely limited.	64-118

5. Sails

The sails are the most important part of any sailboat. What they are made of and how they are handled by the skipper, more than anything else, determine how well and how fast a boat will sail. Thus it is important that you learn something about the parts of sails, how they are made, and how they are used.

Modern mainsails and jibs are made of Dacron, a man-made fiber. Up until the early 1950's, however, sails were made of finely woven Egyptian cotton. We can all be thankful for the discovery that Dacron cloth makes good sails, for it has solved a very serious problem—the need to "break in" a new suit of sails. Cotton sails must be very carefully broken in. They stretch out of shape very easily and do not return to their original shape. Thus, if they are handled carelessly during breaking in, cotton sails can be ruined. They also shrink when they are wet, and are subject to attack by mildew.

Dacron sails, on the other hand, do not suffer to the same extent from any of these shortcomings. Dacron sailcloth is elastic. Thus when it is stretched out of shape it will spring back to its original shape when released, if it has not been subjected to excessive wind force. This allows the sailmaker to cut and sew sails exactly as he wants them. If he is good at his job, the finished sail will set just as he planned it on the drawing board. Dacron sails are not damaged by mildew, which will form on the sail surface. They are, however, affected by some of the chemicals that pollute the air around large cities. In addition, Dacron sails are affected by heat; a live ash from a cigarette or pipe will melt a hole instantly.

As sturdy as Dacron sails are, they can be damaged in heavy

These unusual transparent sails are made of Mylar, a nonwoven synthetic material. They were constructed and raced successfully on Lake Michigan by Bill Hackel of Chicago, Illinois, showing that there is always room for experimentation and improvement of sailboat performance. (Photo by John Fleming)

weather. Not too long ago, while sailing a twenty-four-foot sloop on Long Island Sound, my family and I found ourselves sailing into the teeth of a northwest wind that was gusting to about thirty-five knots. If we hadn't had to get home, we would have been wise to pull into a sheltered harbor to wait the wind out. As it was, we had to tack some fifteen miles into that very strong wind. We furled the mainsail, and tacked using just the working jib until we were right off home port. At this point the waves were running six to eight feet, making it impossible to go forward to lower the jib. As a result, when we switched to power and headed directly into the wind, the jib luffed (flapped) wildly, even though we tried to hold it tight with the sheet lines. This wild luffing caused the sail to tear in several places, showing that as tough as Dacron is, it can be damaged. Sailing in thirty-five-knot winds is not recommended, either. If we had it to do over again, we would head into that sheltered harbor and wait for the wind to go down, regardless of how important it was to get home.

To care for your mainsail properly, don't leave it furled on the boom for long periods of time, unless you protect it with a sail cover. It is much better to stow the main along with the jib in sail bags, or in a dry locker at the yacht club or at home. At the end of the season, if your sails don't require repairs by the sailmaker, you can store them yourself. Simply hose them down with fresh water, fold them neatly after they are dry, and stow them away in their bags in a dry, cool place. If salt has accumulated on the sail, it should be scrubbed off.

MAINSAILS

The mainsail is the principal driving sail on a fore-and-aft-rigged boat. Virtually all small sailboats in use today are fore-and-aft-rigged. They carry one of three types of mainsail: the *jib-headed,* or Marconi; the *gaff-headed;* or the *loose-footed.*

The type of mainsail you will most likely work with is the jib-headed. As the drawing shows, a jib-headed main is long, narrow, and triangular. But it is much more than a large piece of triangular sailcloth. As you learned in Chapter 4, the sail must have a curved shape when set in order for it to drive the boat properly. This curve is called the *draft* of the sail. For light winds, a sail should have a fairly deep draft. In heavy weather it is better for the sail to be flatter in shape. Dedicated racing skippers carry several suits of sails, with varying amounts of draft, to permit them to use the sail that best matches the wind conditions. On good mainsails, the deepest part of the curve of the draft is about one-third the distance from the mast going aft toward the leech. The curve then flattens out to a straight line as it approaches the trailing edge of the sail.

The drawing shows how the draft is produced in a sail. First, the strips of cloth that make up the sail are sewn together. Note how

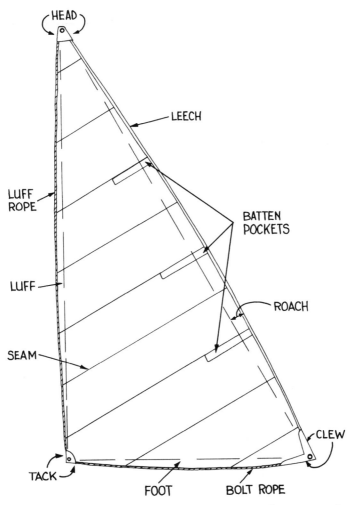

Layout for a jib-headed mainsail. This type of mainsail is easy to handle, and gives the boat more forward drive than the gaff-headed main when sailing to windward.

the seams are at right angles to the line of the leech. Then, when the sail is cut, the luff and the foot are cut along a curve, not on a straight line. The result, when the sail is bent on the straight mast and straight boom, is the draft of the sail. Because the mast and boom are straight, the excess cloth of the curved cuts along the luff and foot appear as the draft. To maintain proper draft, you can see that it is important to keep the mast and boom as straight as possible. This applies to the beginning sailor. Many experts, on the other hand, use a "bendy" rig to good advantage when racing. On a bendy rig, the mast and boom are deliberately bent out of the straight position.

A gaff-headed mainsail is quite different from the jib-headed main. It is a four-sided (quadrilateral) sail with the top edge held aloft by a spar called a *gaff*. Gaff-headed sails are cut shorter on the luff and longer on the foot than jib-headed sails. One reason gaff-headed sails have lost popularity is difficulty of handling. They are heavier than jib-headed sails; the sail itself is much larger, and the gaff also must be hauled aloft. Such sails must be raised by two halyards—one at the peak and one at the throat. Under way, gaff-rigged boats do not sail to windward as efficiently as boats carrying jib-headed sails. Because of their very large sail area, however, gaff-rigged boats usually sail off the wind—reaching and running—much better than their sisters with jib-headed mainsails.

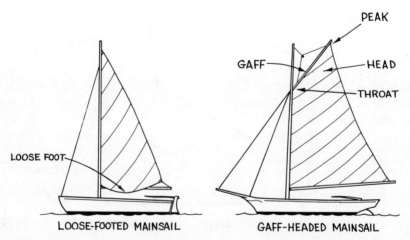

PEAK

GAFF — HEAD

THROAT

LOOSE FOOT

LOOSE-FOOTED MAINSAIL   GAFF-HEADED MAINSAIL

Gaff-headed and loose-footed mainsails. Gaff-rigged boats usually sail very well off the wind because the sail area is so great. Loose-footed mains are often seen on small boats, such as sailing dinghies.

Loose-footed mainsails are similar in shape to jib-headed mains. The foot of the sail, however, is not attached to the boom. Instead, the sail is fastened to the end of the boom by a single line attached to the clew. The set of the sail can be changed by lengthening or shortening the line running from the clew to the end of the boom. The shorter the line, the flatter the sail. Loose-footed mains are usually found on smaller sailboats. For example, certain small dinghies (six to ten feet in length) rigged with the mast stepped well forward, and carrying a mainsail only, use the loose-footed mainsail.

Before moving on to the different types of jibs, let me point out that the parts of sails generally have the same names, even though the sails may be different. Thus, the leading edge of a sail is always the *luff*, and the trailing edge is always the *leech*. The lower edge is always called the *foot*, and the top corner the *head*. The *tack* is the lower corner at the front of the sail, and the *clew* is the lower corner at the trailing edge of the sail. There are slight exceptions to these terms on gaff-rigged mainsails and spinnakers. The drawing shows these exceptions for a gaff main. They will be pointed out for the spinnaker shortly.

JIBS

Old-timers called them *staysails;* today almost everyone calls them *jibs*. The jib is the single sail forward of the mast on a sloop. There are several different types of jib: the *working jib;* the so-called *genoa jib;* the *reaching jib,* or *ballooner;* the *storm jib;* and the *jib topsail*. The working jib and genoa jib are the most important as far as we are concerned. They are in constant use on practically all sailboats, and both will almost certainly be in use on the first sloop-rigged boat you step aboard.

The working jib is a triangular sail usually cut straight on the foot and on the leech. As mentioned, the jib is rigged forward of the mast. It fits within the triangle formed by the deck, the mast, and the jibstay. On most jibs, a strong but light cable called the *luff wire* is sewn into the luff of the sail. The luff wire ends in loops at the head and tack of the sail. Thus, when the jib is raised, it cannot be overstretched. Quite the contrary, many careless sailors fail to tighten the luff wire enough when they raise the jib. When this happens, the sail sags between the jib snaps along the luff, producing a kind of scalloped effect. The jib does not work well when set up this way, for it must be perfectly smooth from luff to leech for maximum efficiency. A good rule of thumb when raising the jib is to tighten the luff wire just enough to produce a slight slack in the jibstay. This will usually guarantee enough tension in the luff wire.

The jib has several important functions. Most important, it creates a driving force, thus helping to push the boat through the water. In addition, when it is set properly with respect to the mainsail, it enhances the driving force of the main. As you recall, it is the wind "slot effect" of a well-set jib that increases the drive of the main. The jib also smoothes the flow of the wind, and it assists in the steering of a sailboat by acting to balance the forces on the boat.

A taut luff wire guarantees that the jib will have its proper shape. But more important than that, if the jib is not set up properly the skipper loses one of his best indications that the boat is sailing cor-

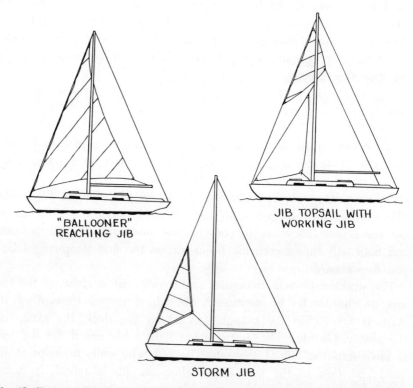

"BALLOONER"
REACHING JIB

JIB TOPSAIL WITH
WORKING JIB

STORM JIB

The "ballooner" is often used on larger boats for reaching in light winds. The jib topsail is set above another jib. It is rarely seen on small sloops. A small working jib made from sturdy material, the storm jib finds use in very heavy weather.

THE SANDBAGGER

The sandbagger, developed during the 1850s, is one of the most in-teresting racing yachts ever contrived. Extremely fast, sandbaggers were very wide and shallow. They carried an enormous amount of sail area on an expanded rig. The boats ran from eighteen to twenty-eight feet in length, and carried a bowsprit almost as long as the hull and a main boom that extended ten feet or more beyond the stern. Under sail, sandbaggers were extremely unstable. As a result, when they were raced they carried twenty-five or more bags of sand in the cockpit as ballast. When a boat came about, a crew of husky men quickly shifted the bags of sand to the windward side. The boat shown here is *Shadow;* it was built in 1895. The rig shown is considerably smaller than the racing rig. (Photo by Peter Barlow)

rectly. When sheeted in properly, the jib will be quietly full at the luff, assuring the skipper that he is getting the best he can out of his sails. On the other hand, the luff of the jib may shiver gently, or even shake violently, depending upon how the sail is sheeted in with respect to the wind. As you gain experience at the helm, you will learn to make frequent checks of the luff of the jib. More than anything else, it will help you set the sails on your boat properly.

People often hear the term "working sails" applied to the mainsail and a small jib. This term goes back to the days when fishing boats and other work boats were powered by sail alone. This combination of jib and mainsail was the easiest to handle on such boats, hence the term "working sails."

The genoa jib is a much larger sail, also triangular in shape. It gets its name from a similarity to a sail used by fishermen near the city of Genoa, Italy. As the drawing shows, genoa jibs have a very long foot; they overlap the mainsail, and must be sheeted way aft. As a result, they have to be set outside the shrouds.

Because of their greater area, and because they form a longer and more definite slot between main and jib, genoa jibs supply more drive than working jibs. Almost all of the larger cruising type sailboats carry genoa jibs; many smaller boats do also. The genoa jib is used to obtain more speed when the wind is light enough to make the working jib

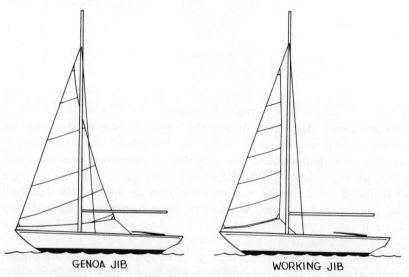

GENOA JIB   WORKING JIB

The most widely used headsails, the working jib and genoa jib add drive and ease of handling to a sailboat.

ineffective. Genoas are primarily used for beating and for close reaching. They become quite difficult to handle when the wind is astern, although you will occasionally see a boat running before the wind with a small genoa jib set "wing-and-wing" with a mainsail.

As you can readily see, the enormous area of a genoa jib makes it difficult to handle. When filled with wind, such jibs pull so hard on the sheet line they must be sheeted in with the help of a *winch*. Winches, you recall, are simple wheel-and-axle devices that make it easier to pull in a heavy load. But this strong pull on the sheet line isn't the only problem the skipper and crew face when a genoa jib is in use. If through carelessness the skipper finds himself in too strong a wind for safe sailing, his boat may be in danger of capsizing. Wise skippers learn early in the game just how much wind their boats can take when a genoa is in use. The foolish sailors often get a sudden and violent dunking.

Coming about with a genoa jib on the boat is not as simple or quick as it is with a working jib. First, the clew of the sail must come forward past the shrouds and around the mast. While this is taking place, there is a danger that the sheet line or the sail itself will snag. Thus it is often necessary for a crew member to carry the clew forward around the mast. All of this means that the tack has to be performed much more slowly than with a working jib. It can't be done too slowly, though, or the boat may go into "irons"—that is, the boat may stall and lose headway, with the sails luffing, halfway through the coming-about maneuver.

Look back at the diagram of a jib-headed mainsail and note the extra sail area along the leech called the *roach*. The extra material of the roach adds drive to the sail when reaching or running before the wind. But the roach is apt to curl or flap if it isn't supported. This support is supplied by long, narrow slats called *battens*. Made of wood, plastic, or aluminum, battens are slipped into pockets sewn into the sail. Batten pockets should be one to two inches longer than the battens they hold. In addition to use on mainsails, battens are often used on working jibs. Their effect once again is to support and smooth the trailing edge of the sail.

If battens are made and fitted to a sail correctly, they will bend to the shape of the sail and form a smooth curve. This allows the wind to flow over the sail with no interruption. A batten that is too stiff, however, forms a sharp bend in the sail, and obstructs the smooth flow of the wind.

You can save yourself a lot of trouble with broken and lost battens if you follow a few simple rules. Insert battens carefully to avoid tearing the pocket seams. When fully inserted, be sure the batten is either tied securely or locked into the pocket (see the drawing). It is also advisable to remove the battens when the sail is furled or packed away into a bag. A broken batten does little good and may poke through the sail. A batten that has flown out of its pocket, only to sink or float away from the boat, is also useless.

THE SPINNAKER

Very few sights on the water can equal the sheer beauty of a sailboat running before the wind with its spinnaker set perfectly. If possible, an even more awe-inspiring sight is a fleet of competing cruising-class sailboats, all with their spinnakers set and lifting. Perhaps you've had the good fortune to witness such a racing fleet emerge from the horizon on, say, Long Island Sound, San Francisco Bay, or Lake Michigan. It's a sight to remember. Although the majority of sails are white, spinnakers are usually multicolored in a variety of different geometric designs, adding to the spectacle as the fleet passes by.

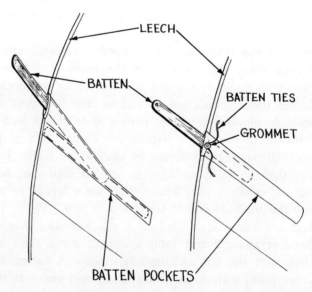

Battens prevent the trailing edge of a sail from curling or flapping in the wind.

The modern spinnaker is used for reaching and for sailing before the wind. Spinnakers vary considerably in shape, depending on such factors as the design of the boat and the ideas of sailmakers and skippers. Thus, you may see long, narrow spinnakers, as well as round, egg-, and bell-shaped ones. Because the sail is used a great deal in light winds, it is made from very light but very strong nylon fabric. If you've been observant, you've noticed that many spinnakers are dark in color at the top of the sail but light in color at the bottom. There's a reason for this. Some people feel that the dark fabric absorbs heat from the sun, and then warms the air beneath it inside the upper portion of the sail. Warm air, of course, rises. Thus, this warming effect gives greater lift to the sail, helping to hold it up where it belongs in very light winds.

Spinnakers are not easy to set, nor are they easy to control once they are flying. But more about this later. Look at the diagram of a spinnaker in position. The top corner of the sail is the *head* and the bottom edge, the *foot*. Unlike other sails, both side edges are called *leeches*, and both lower corners are called *clews*. On the windward side of the boat, opposite the mainsail, a *spinnaker boom* or *pole* is rigged from the mast to the clew of the sail. The corner of the sail the spinnaker pole is attached to is called the *tack*, but only while the pole is rigged this way. The side edge of the sail above the tack is then called the *luff*. Often, however, it is necessary to change the course of the boat, requiring that the mainsail and the spinnaker pole be shifted to the opposite side of the boat. This tactic is called *jibing the spinnaker*. It will be explained later. The important thing to note here is that when the spinnaker is jibed, the tack and luff of the sail also move over to the other side.

The spinnaker is controlled by several lines. It is raised by the spinnaker halyard and held in position by several other lines. The sheet line is attached to the loose, hanging corner of the sail, the clew. The other corner, the tack, is usually controlled by three separate lines. One of these, the *topping lift*, runs from the mast to the spinnaker pole. In addition, an *after guy* runs from the outer end of the spinnaker pole back to the cockpit, and a *forward guy* runs to the foredeck and then back to the cockpit. The topping lift and guy lines permit the crew to move the tack of the spinnaker up and down and forward and aft. To be effective, the spinnaker must be very carefully adjusted to the frequent wind shifts that seem to occur when a boat is sailing downwind. It takes a highly skilled and coordinated crew to do this job well.

Spinnakers, despite their great efficiency and beauty, can cause serious trouble at times. For example, because the nylon fabric used is very light, it may tear in heavy winds. More than one skipper, trying to make up lost time in a wind too heavy for a spinnaker, has watched in chagrin as the wind has torn the sail to shreds. The tattered fragment left at the masthead makes a fine, if very expensive, wind pennant. Sometimes, too, the spinnaker can fly out of control as it is being set or jibed. When this happens the sail usually wraps itself around the jibstay. Needless to say, it is very difficult to un-tangle this kind of snarl-up. Smart skippers try to prevent this problem by rigging a harness between the jibstay and mast that serves to block the spinnaker as it begins to curl around the jibstay. It helps also to have a crew that knows what it is doing. Beautiful, efficient, but tricky and full of surprises; this, in a nutshell, sums up the spinnaker.

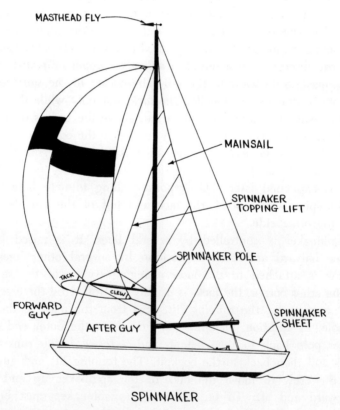

SPINNAKER

A spinnaker in position and lifting. It takes a great deal of practice to master use of the spinnaker.

6. Rigging

Having completed our discussion of sails and how they harness the wind's energy to drive a sailboat, we must now look into rigging—the *shrouds, stays,* and *lines* that support and control the sails and spars. As you will soon see, the rigging has a great deal to do with a boat's performance. Thus you must understand what it does and how it is handled.

STANDING RIGGING

The rigging used to support the mast is called standing rigging. As the drawing of one possible arrangement shows, the standing rigging consists of several different stays and shrouds. Shrouds support the mast at its sides, and stays support it fore and aft. Let's first consider the stays and what they accomplish. The rig shown is called a seven-eighths rig because the *jibstay* ends about seven-eighths of the distance up the mast. As you can see, it ties into the mast somewhat below the backward pull of the permanent *backstay*. On some boats you will see *running backstays* instead of a permanent backstay. When the boat is under sail, beating to windward, the pressure on the mainsail pulls the top of the mast aft. At the same time, the jib is pulling the mast forward at the point where the jibstay is tied in. You now see why the *jumper struts* and *jumper stays* are necessary. Without them, the combined effects of the mainsail and jib would tend to bend the top of the mast aft.

Modern boats are usually equipped with lightweight stainless steel stays and shrouds. Stainless steel wire has enormous strength for its weight. It also resists corrosion, and although it does stretch some, this is not usually a critical problem if the stretch is taken into account when tuning the rig.

In general, the beginning sailor is better off keeping his mast straight. More often than not, this means straight up and down and centered exactly. It is the shrouds that hold the mast straight and in the center of the boat. The mast should not lean or bow either to starboard or port. The drawing shows how the shrouds prevent bowing in the mast.

Note that there are two sets of shrouds, upper and lower. The upper shrouds pass over the spreader and support the top of the mast. Under sail, the strain on the upper shroud on the windward side thrusts against the mast through the spreader. This tends to make the mast bow to leeward. To prevent such bowing, the lower windward shrouds are attached to the mast at the base of the spreader. As you can

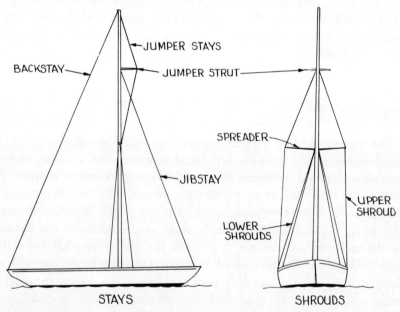

STAYS   SHROUDS

Standing rigging on a typical sloop. As you can see, when they are adjusted properly the shrouds and stays hold the mast exactly in position.

see, the combined effect of the two shrouds is to hold the mast perfectly straight.

One problem every sailor faces is tuning his rig; that is, finding the combination of mast rake (tip forward or aft) and tautness of stays and shrouds that gives the best sailing performance. Unfortunately,

THE SCHOONER *Bowdoin*

The only schooner in America today that was specifically designed for arctic exploration, the *Bowdoin* was launched in 1921. She made twenty-six polar expeditions in all, sailing over three hundred thousand miles. The ship is named for Bowdoin College, the school of her owner, Admiral Donald B. MacMillan. In 1909 MacMillan was with Peary, another Bowdoin College graduate, when the North Pole was discovered. The *Bowdoin* is an unusual schooner in many respects. She is short-rigged for heavy weather and carries no topmast or bowsprit. Her bow carries an 1800-pound piece of steel plate to protect against heavy ice, and is spoon-shaped so that she can ride up on ice that can't be broken through. The hull is double framed to resist the enormous pressure of pack ice. Still seaworthy, the *Bowdoin* now rests in retirement at Camden, Maine.

there are no set rules for tuning. Indeed, there are probably as many theories of tuning as there are sailors. Some prefer the standing rigging to be set up "bar taut," while others insist that slack rigging makes a boat go best.

For the beginning sailor, there is an intermediate choice that will produce good performance with relatively little difficulty. To begin with, the mast must be straight as well as *athwartships* (directly above the centerline of the boat) at all times. Obviously, the base of the mast must be securely fastened in its proper position. If it should slip, the entire mast would be out of alignment. The next step is to adjust the shrouds so that the mast stands straight. This is accomplished by means of *turnbuckles*, which are fastened to *chain plates*. On most boats, chain plates are metal straps that run down the side of the hull. They are securely fastened through the hull or deck. You can make certain the mast is centered properly by measuring the distance between the masthead and a similar point on each side of the boat. The two distances, of course, should be equal. The best way to make this measurement is to attach a steel tape measure to the shackle of the main halyard, and then run the shackle up to the masthead.

Finally, it is necessary to adjust the shrouds so that the mast remains straight while under sail. This is the most difficult part of tuning. You will have to take your boat out to check the mast carefully while on several different points of sailing on both tacks. With a reliable crew member at the helm, crawl forward and sight up the mast. If it is bending or leaning to leeward, take up on the windward shrouds until it is straight. If the mast is out of line toward the windward side, loosen the windward shrouds. Once the rig is tuned properly, you will find the leeward shrouds a bit slack, while the windward shrouds are taut. Then, when the boat is on the other tack, the reverse will occur. That is, regardless of whether you are on a starboard or a port tack, the windward shrouds will be taut and the leeward shrouds slightly slack, but the mast will be perfectly straight.

In general, the upper shrouds—those leading to the masthead—should be fairly taut. The lower shrouds should be somewhat less taut than the upper shrouds. This builds in a compensation for stretch in the longer upper shrouds. If the lowers are set up as taut as the uppers, stretch in the uppers will allow the masthead to bend to leeward when the rig is under tension.

Finally, it is necessary to adjust the fore-and-aft position of the masthead. The wisest thing to do here is to follow your boat's sail plan. That is, set the rake of the mast according to the designer's plan. If the design is a good one, this position should produce a satisfactory helm when the boat is going to windward. If it turns out that the boat does not have good balance, that is, that it has excessive *weather helm* or *lee helm,* adjustment in the rake of the mast may help. This will be discussed in greater detail in Chapter 8.

Both the jibstay (or headstay) and the backstay must be set up quite taut. If your boat has jumper stays, as in the drawing, these should be tightened enough to bend the top of the mast slightly forward before the mast is stepped. The mast will then straighten when the backstay is taken up. There are good reasons for taut stays. If the jibstay is slack, the luff of the jib will sag to leeward. This greatly reduces the jib's efficiency going to windward. If the backstay is slack, on the other hand, the weight of the jib will pull the mast

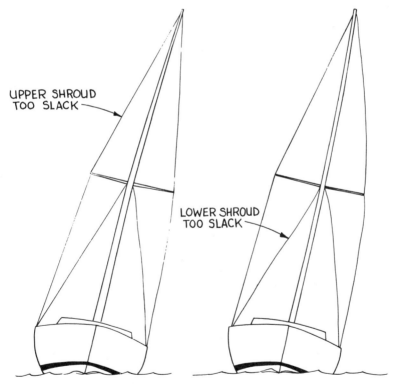

How improper adjustment of the shrouds affects the mast. It bows or bends to leeward when the lower shroud is too slack, and it bows or bends to windward when the upper shroud is too slack.

forward, and the set of the mainsail will be disturbed. As you recall, the average mainsail is cut for use with a straight mast. If the mast should bend or twist, the sail's shape is altered. Wrinkles then occur, as well as *hard spots*—areas of the sail that are stretched flat, not properly curved.

Despite anything that you might read in a book, however, the real test of a tuning job is in the sailing. There is simply no way other than a careful and thorough tuning *under sail* to get the most out of a boat. Many sailors, dissatisfied with their boats, can lay the blame in their own laps for failing to properly tune their rigs.

RUNNING RIGGING

By removing all of the remaining rigging from the drawing, we have shown just the running rigging. The principal lines in the running rigging are the *halyards,* which pull sails up, and the *sheet lines,* which pull sails in. In addition, there is the *topping lift,* which holds the boom up when the mainsail has been lowered, and the *outhaul,* which pulls the foot of the mainsail taut along the boom. Finally, *downhauls* pull sails down into positions that produce more effective drive. When a spinnaker is in use, you recall, one of the controlling lines is a *guy line.*

Sheet lines control the position of the sails relative to the wind. Sails may be sheeted in tightly, as when sailing to windward, or sheeted way out, as when running before the wind. There are two problems related to the sheet lines. First, just how much line must be eased out to get the greatest efficiency from the sails? This we will discuss later. Second, where on the boat should the sheet lines lead? Let's consider the jibsheets first.

As the drawing shows, the jibsheets are led to the deck along a line that makes a ten-degree angle from the centerline of the boat. On most boats, the jibsheet block is fastened to a slide on a track along this line. Thus the problem is one of positioning the slide to get the best performance from the jib.

To find out where the lead should be for your boat, sail the boat as close to the wind as you can, and then very gradually start to *luff up* (head into the wind). If the jibsheet lead is correctly positioned, the jib will luff, that is, begin to flap, along the entire forward edge of the sail. If the jib should luff nearer the foot of the sail first,

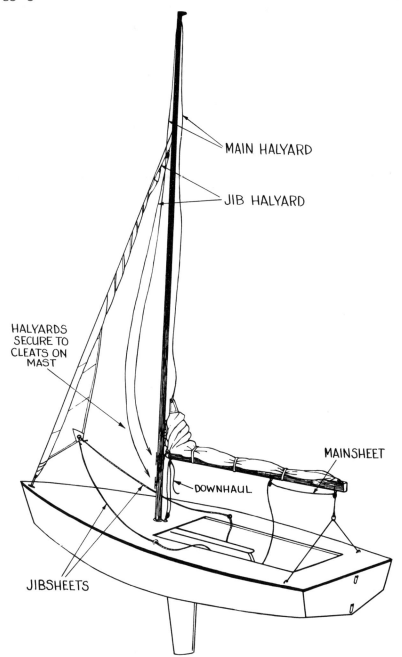

MAIN HALYARD

JIB HALYARD

HALYARDS
SECURE TO
CLEATS ON
MAST

MAINSHEET

DOWNHAUL

JIBSHEETS

With all other gear and rigging removed, it is easy to identify the various parts of the running rigging.

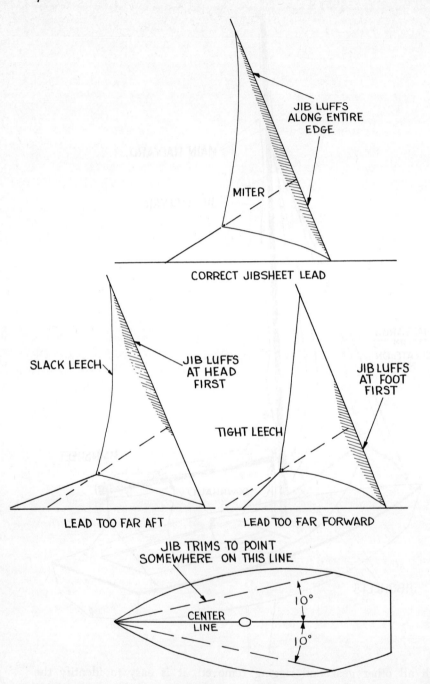

JIB LUFFS
ALONG ENTIRE
EDGE

MITER

CORRECT JIBSHEET LEAD

SLACK LEECH

JIB LUFFS
AT HEAD
FIRST

TIGHT LEECH

JIB LUFFS
AT FOOT
FIRST

LEAD TOO FAR AFT

LEAD TOO FAR FORWARD

JIB TRIMS TO POINT
SOMEWHERE ON THIS LINE

10°

CENTER
LINE

10°

Correct trim for the jibsheet lead. When the lead is too far forward,
a tight leech will backwind the main. When the lead is too far aft,
a slack leech flutters and interferes with smooth airflow.

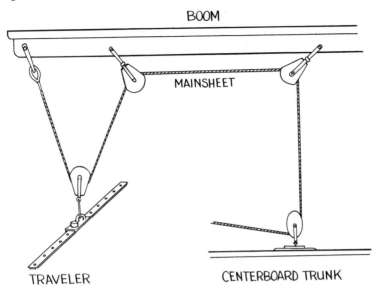

BOOM

MAINSHEET

TRAVELER   CENTERBOARD TRUNK

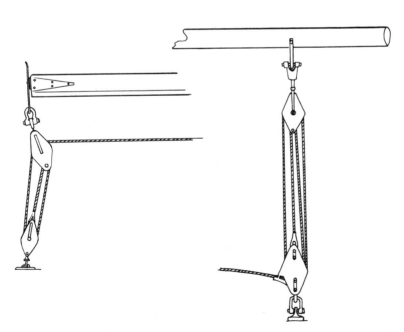

Three typical mainsheet lead arrangements. The one at bottom left is used on roller reefing booms, which must be rotated to take up sail.

the lead is too far forward; move the block aft on the track. If the jib should luff nearer the head of the sail first, the lead is too far aft; move the block forward on the track.

There are many different possibilities for rigging the mainsheet. We show three popular arrangements in the drawing. If you look carefully the next time you are in a well-populated harbor, you will see numerous others. How the mainsheet is rigged, however, is less important than how it is used, for the mainsail must be trimmed correctly for maximum efficiency.

When sailing to windward, it is important that the full length of the luff of the main enter the wind at the same angle. Unfortunately, this does not occur perfectly because the upper part of the sail twists away from the wind. But with the head sagging off this way, less sail area is available for generating drive. It's impossible to completely correct this condition, but it can be improved greatly by changing

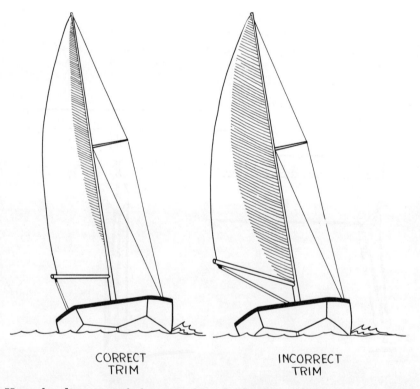

CORRECT
TRIM

INCORRECT
TRIM

How the direction of the mainsheet lead affects the sail when sailing to windward. When the boom is trimmed out and down, the sail flattens and greater drive is generated.

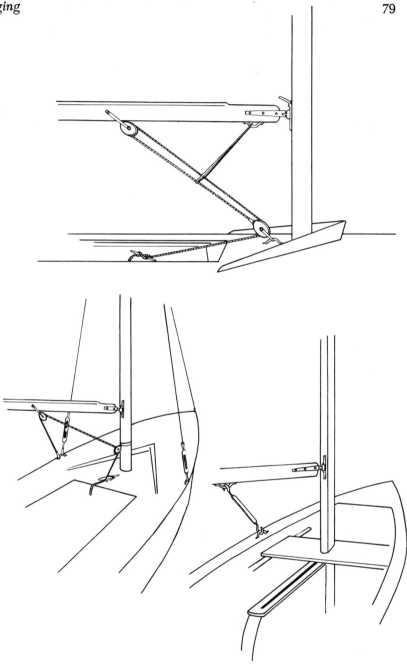

Three possible boom vang arrangements. While these rigs are clearly different, they all have the same function—holding the boom down while on a broad reach or running so that the sail does not sag off at the head.

the direction of the pull of the mainsheet in relation to the center-line of the boat.

As the drawing shows, a pull downward on the boom has a flattening effect on the sail. This is what is desired. On the other hand, when the boom is sheeted in on an angle, the end of the boom tends to rise, and the head of the sail sags off. For windward work, then, the rule is trim the boom out-and-down. On many boats the sheet block is attached to a traveler (a track) that permits this adjustment. The crew simply slides the block outward away from the centerline of the boat.

When beating in light air, however, a different arrangement is necessary. Under these circumstances, more draft in the sail is required than when sailing closehauled in medium or heavy wind. This additional draft can be produced by moving the mainsheet block in toward the centerline of the boat, thus permitting the boom to lift somewhat. Easing off the clew outhaul a bit helps the situation also.

When reaching or running in winds other than very light airs, however, the mainsail should be fairly flat to achieve the best possible performance. Unfortunately, the sheet line is of no help here, for when the boom is trimmed way out, the sheet line pulls in rather than down. Thus some other rig must be used to hold the boom down.

A *boom vang* solves the problem. As the drawing shows, there are a number of different ways to do the job. It's important, however, to be sure the vang rig will go on and come off easily, with little or no chance of tangling. You should also remember that a boom vang puts an enormous strain on the boom, gooseneck fitting, and mast. It should be designed and installed by someone who knows what he is doing.

7. Marlinspike Seamanship

A marlinspike is a pointed wood or steel wedge used to open strands of rope and wire for splicing. And splicing, of course, is one of the important ways to join two pieces of rope or wire. Needless to say, many different types of objects are fastened together on a boat. In general, rope is used for these fastenings. Over a period of many hundreds of years, the use of rope on board a boat has come to be known as marlinspike seamanship. It's important that you learn some of these fundamentals, for without them you will find handling a sailboat a difficult task. The skills of marlinspike seamanship require practice. Many sailors find practicing knots and splices during the winter a worthwhile pastime. It helps to keep one's skills in top shape and also to make the long winter easier to get through.

What is rope? In all ropes that are not braided, *fibers* are twisted to the right to form *yarns*, yarns are twisted to the left to form *strands*, and strands are twisted to the right to form *ropes*. Such ropes are said to be laid right-handed. They must be coiled clockwise to avoid kinks and twists. Try it for yourself. Coil a piece of rope both clockwise and counterclockwise. What happens when you pull rope off the coil in each instance?

Of the ropes in general use on boats today, two are of plant origin and two are synthetic. Manila and sisal are the natural fiber ropes, and nylon and Dacron are the synthetics. There are great advantages to nylon and Dacron ropes, which accounts for why you see them in use on so many boats. They are more costly than Manila or sisal, but their advantages far outweigh the additional cost.

Nylon rope has a very high elasticity and great strength for its weight. Thus it is very useful for anchor, mooring, and docking lines, as well as for towing lines. Its elasticity provides a built-in spring that absorbs many of the jolts and sharp tugs a boat encounters at anchor or tied up to a dock. Its great strength, of course, allows the use of a much lighter and less bulky line for most jobs. In addition, nylon fiber is waterproof and highly resistant to rot. It can be stowed away while still wet, an impossibility with Manila or sisal, both of which are subject to rot.

Handle nylon rope that is under tension with great respect. Its elasticity makes it a threat to the safety of the unwary. A stretched nylon tow line can tear free and snap back with alarming suddenness and great force. It pays to stand clear of any nylon tow line.

Dacron rope has less strength than nylon, but it has the advantage

These sailors are hiking out to prevent excessive heel during a beat to windward on Cape Cod waters. Notice the good "slot effect." (Photo by Dorothy I. Crossley)

of a very low elasticity. Thus it finds use in halyards and sheet lines, where stretching is undesirable. Dacron rope is very easy to work, being soft, pliable, and easy on the hands.

Up to this point we have been talking about rope. The sailor uses rope for many things, but he generally refers to it as *line* when it is in use on board a boat. Line may be fastened to itself, another line, or to some object. This is where *knots, bends,* and *hitches* come in. Knots are used to bind objects together or to secure a bundle or package. A hitch is used to secure a line to another object, and a bend joins two line ends to each other. You must know certain knots, hitches, and bends before venturing out by yourself on a boat. There are few things more embarrassing than the mishap that sometimes occurs because a knot, hitch, or bend is improperly tied.

Of the knots, three are an absolute must. These are the *reef* (or *square*) knot, the *figure-eight* knot, and the *bowline*. The drawing shows how these knots are tied. The square knot serves many purposes: lashing objects to the deck, tying in battens, reefing, fastening down sail covers, and so on. Be careful, though, to tie the square knot correctly. The incorrect version, the *granny* knot, slips easily. In addition, never use the square knot as a bend—that is, to tie two ropes together. Almost certainly the knot will slip.

The figure eight is useful as a *stopper* knot. Tie it into the free end of sheet lines and halyards to prevent them from running out through the blocks or fairleads should the line get away from you. Avoid the simple overhand knot, though. It tends to jam, and it is difficult to untie.

The bowline is the single most important knot of the sailor. It is used to fasten a line to an object or to put a loop at the end of a line. Its most important advantage is that it will never slip, nor will it ever jam. A properly tied bowline is very simple to release once the tension has been taken off. The drawing shows how to tie a bowline. The first step is to make a small loop in the line, leaving enough line free to make a loop of the desired size. The free end is then passed through the small loop as shown, under the standing part, and back through the small loop. You should learn how to tie a bowline blindfolded. The day (or night) may come when you will be glad you did.

84

Hitches, as we mentioned, are used to secure a line to an object. For example, one might wish to fasten a line to a pile, a bitt, a spar, or a ring. Often, for strictly temporary tying up, a clove hitch is used to fasten a docking line to a pile. Under no circumstances should a clove hitch be regarded as secure or permanent. A clove hitch pulls out quite easily if it is subjected to tugs and pulls from different directions.

A more secure hitch is the familar two half hitches. More people than not tie two half hitches without realizing exactly what they are doing. This is a useful and important hitch. It is often used by itself, but also finds use as a safety hitch. For example, the clove hitch can be made more secure by half-hitching the line's end to its standing part.

No sailor can get by without knowing how to fasten a line to a

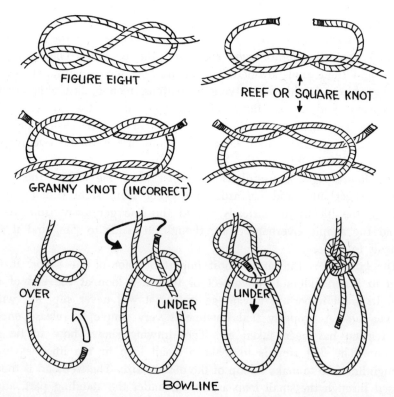

FIGURE EIGHT

REEF OR SQUARE KNOT

GRANNY KNOT (INCORRECT)

OVER   UNDER   UNDER

BOWLINE

Knots bind objects together, or secure a package. These knots (with the exception of the "granny") are essential to the sailor.

cleat. Thus the cleat hitch must be learned—and correctly. A quick look at how a sailor ties his cleat hitches will tell you more about his ability as a seaman than any other skill. Look closely the next time you wander around a marina. Some of the "rat's nests" passing for cleat hitches are appalling. Moreover, they are apt to pull out. It's *how* you fasten a line to a cleat, not how many turns you wrap on, that counts.

Many inexperienced sailors make the mistake of using the wrong kind of fastening to attach two line ends to each other. The correct fastening is the sheet bend. The drawing shows two types of sheet bend: the double sheet bend for fastening light line to heavy line, and the ordinary sheet bend, used to connect lines with nearly the same diameter. The other fastening shown—the fisherman's bend—is not really a bend. It is a hitch. Sailors insist on calling it a bend,

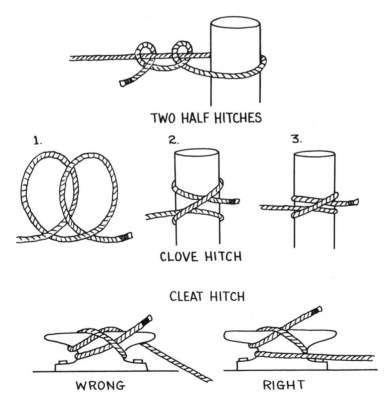

TWO HALF HITCHES

1.   2.   3.

CLOVE HITCH

CLEAT HITCH

WRONG   RIGHT

Hitches fasten a line to an object. When tying a boat up, be sure to use the proper hitch, and be doubly sure it is properly tied.

however, so we will also. The fisherman's bend is used to fasten the anchor line to the ring or shackle of your anchor. It is a quick, easy, and secure substitute for an eye splice made around a thimble. The two turns of the fisherman's bend around the ring or shackle will wear, however, so the bend should be inspected and retied occasionally.

WHIPPING

Another clue to the seamanship ability of a sailor is the condition of the ends of his lines. If his lines are unraveling at their ends, or if they have bulky knots tied into the ends to prevent unraveling, you can be sure of questionable seamanship skills. The lines of a good seaman are neatly and properly whipped.

There are several ways to whip a line end in this day of synthetic materials. With the introduction of waterproof tapes, for example, some sailors have taken to using tape whipping. This is a good temporary whipping, but should be replaced with something more permanent, for sooner or later the tape slips off. Another modern whipping consists of

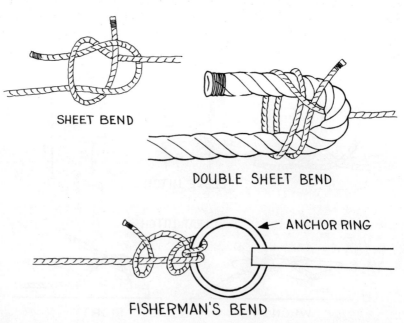

SHEET BEND

DOUBLE SHEET BEND

ANCHOR RING

FISHERMAN'S BEND

Bends fasten two line ends to each other. The fisherman's "bend"— really a hitch—is a useful way to fasten anchor line to anchor ring.

a plastic sleeve slightly larger in diameter than the line to be whipped. The sleeve is slipped into place and then heated with a match or lighter flame. The plastic shrinks up tight when heated and stays tight after cooling. A useful trick when nylon or Dacron line is being whipped is burning the end of the line with a flame. The synthetic melts and fuses, forming a small knob of greater diameter at the end of the line. This prevents unraveling and holds the whipping in place.

The more traditional whipping consists of some form of light, strong cord wrapped around the end of the line. Sailmaker's thread, waxed sail twine, or even stout nylon thread may be used. The drawing shows the easiest of the traditional whippings—the common whipping. Other whippings are more difficult to do, but last longer than common whipping.

SPLICES

A final skill with rope required of all sailors is the art of splicing. There are many different types of splices for the dedicated seaman to learn. For our purposes, however, two will suffice. These are the *eye splice*, for forming a permanent loop, and the *short splice*, for permanently joining two pieces of line of equal diameter. The short splice is quite easy, but it will not pass through a block or fairlead because it doubles

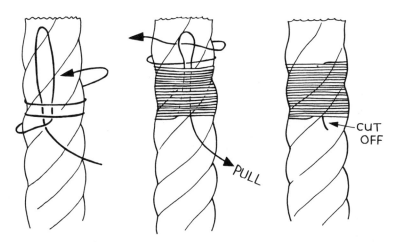

The common whipping is the easiest to apply, although it does not stand up as well as the more elaborate cord whippings.

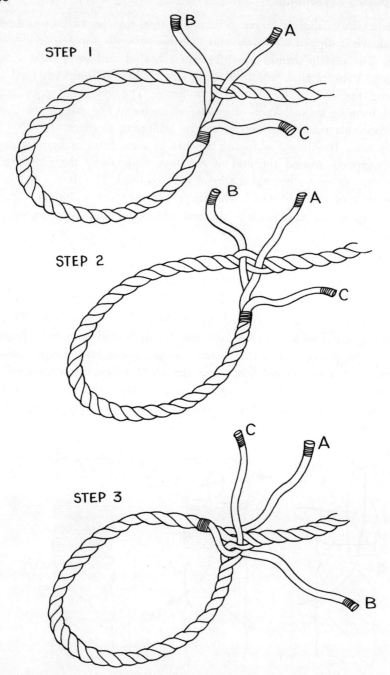

STEP 1

STEP 2

STEP 3

The eye splice is a must for the sailor. Numerous lines aboard a boat call for the neatly looped end produced by an eye splice.

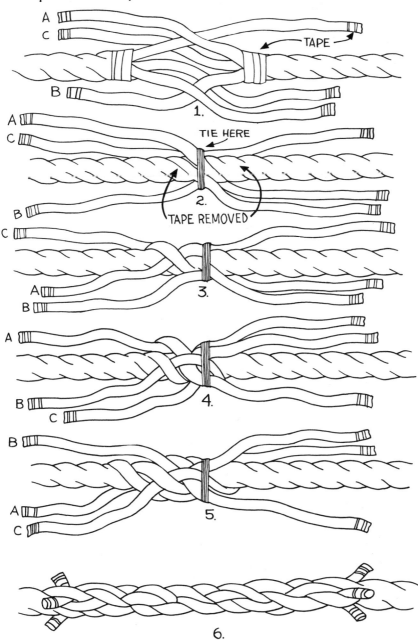

The short splice permanently joins two line ends together. It doubles the volume of the line, however, and will not pass through a block or fairlead.

the diameter of the line. If the line must pass through a block, the *long splice* must be used.

The drawing shows how an eye splice is made. The first step is to unwind three strands to a length of about eight inches. Tightly tape the line at the base of the unwound portion, and also tape the ends of the strands. In an eye splice, the first series of tucks is the most difficult, so follow the drawing carefully. First, push the middle strand A under one of the strands on the standing part. Next, pass B over the strand that A went under and tuck it under the next strand to the left. Note that all tucks go from right to left. Finally, turn the splice over and tuck C from right to left under the strand that lies between A and B. Now pull the tucks tight, and start the next series of tucks. From this point on, A, B, and C each go over their next strand and under the following strand. For manila line, three to four tucks is enough. For nylon line you should put in six or seven tucks to compensate for the slipperiness of the material. Remove the tape from the loop before smoothing out the splice.

The approach to the short splice is the same as in the eye splice—all tucks go over one and under one from right to left against the lay of the strands. First, tape each piece of line about eight inches from the ends and at the end of each of the strands. Next, run the two pieces of line together as shown in steps 1 and 2, and tie them together tightly where they join. The tapes can now be removed. Make your first tuck as shown in step 3, going from right to left with strand A. Then rotate the splice and make the next tuck with strand B, as shown in step 4. Step 5 shows the third and last tuck, using strand C. Now continue on in turn, and make two additional series of tucks. This completes half the splice.

The other half of the splice is started by turning the line around in your lap. Complete three tucks with each strand, and pound and roll the splice on a hard surface to evenly distribute the strands and smooth out the splice. Both the short splice and the eye splice are completed by cutting away the excess and then whipping the end of each strand.

8. Wind, Water, and Sail

Earlier, when we explained how the wind drives a sailboat, we used such terms as *beating, reaching,* and *running.* These terms describe the basic sailing positions relative to the wind. Up to this point it was enough for you to have just a general idea of what they mean. Now it becomes necessary to look more closely at their meanings, for in the next chapter we will be embarking on an imaginary sail. For both this imaginary sail and the real sailing you will do later, a greater knowledge of how the wind and a boat interact is necessary.

The drawing shows the positions of the boat and the sail settings relative to the wind for all courses on the *starboard tack*. When a boat is on the starboard tack, the wind is coming in over the starboard side of the boat. For the *port tack*—wind coming in over the port side of the boat—just picture the mirror image of the diagram. All of the positions for the port tack are exactly opposite those shown.

Sailboats are sailed either *to windward* or *to leeward*. Whenever the bow of the boat is more into the wind than away from the wind, it is sailing to windward. Beating and close reaching are windward courses. The dividing line is the beam reach; when a boat is on a beam reach, the wind is at right angles to the course of the boat. Finally, when the bow of the boat is away from the wind, the boat is sailing to leeward. Broad reaching and running are leeward courses.

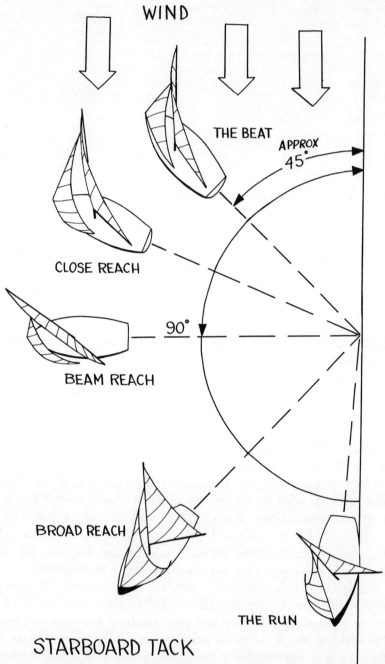

WIND

THE BEAT

APPROX 45°

CLOSE REACH

90°

BEAM REACH

BROAD REACH

THE RUN

STARBOARD TACK

The basic sailing positions, and how they relate to the direction of the wind. Reaching is probably the most exciting point of sailing.

BEATING

When a boat is beating, it is sailing as close to the wind as possible—but usually not closer than forty-five degrees to the wind direction. Sailing closehauled requires careful attention to several details. As you recall, the main boom is trimmed down-and-out to the lee quarter in order to flatten the mainsail. The jib is sheeted in carefully to produce the best possible slot effect. This is the position of sailing with the greatest sideways effect of the wind's energy; hence it is often necessary to climb up and out on the windward side of the boat to counteract heeling. This is called "hiking out." Several of the pictures in the book show you that hiking out can sometimes be quite an acrobatic stunt.

In order to find the course for beating—that is, to get as close to the wind as possible without luffing—follow these steps. Sheet in the mainsail and jib, and slowly head up into the wind until the mainsail luffs (flaps, or backwinds). Then ease off until the luffing stops. This is your course. The sails should be full and drawing well. If you are holding course, but the sail begins to luff, it means the wind has shifted ahead—that is, it has *hauled.* Fall off until the luffing stops. If you suspect that the wind has shifted more toward the stern—that is, has *veered*—head up into the wind until the sail begins to luff. Easing off until the luffing stops then gives you the new course.

When beating, it is important to check the condition of the boat constantly. For example, if you seem to be going too slowly, fall off a bit. It's possible to point too close to the wind; this costs speed. You might also try easing the sheets a bit, because pinching will also slow a boat. Always keep an eye on the forward third of the mainsail. This is where luffing first occurs; it therefore tells you wind direction at once.

REACHING

In general, there are three reaching positions: the *close reach,* the *beam reach,* and the *broad reach.* All lie between beating and running before the wind. In many respects, reaching gives the sailor the most fun for his efforts. The boat usually heels less on a reach than when beating, and goes faster because a greater portion of the total wind force goes into drive. In addition, the boat is usually in better balance on a reach. As a result, handling is easier.

On a beam reach the wind is approximately at right angles to the course of the boat. As you can see, beam reaching is fast and thrilling sailing. (Photo by Dorothy I. Crossley)

This Geary 18 sloop, representative of a class well known on the West Coast, is running before the wind with the sails set wing-and-wing. (Photo by Fred Milke Photographers)

The close reach lies between the beat and the broad reach. To set the sails for a close reach, first put the boat on course. Then ease out the sheets until both the mainsail and jib begin to luff. At this point, haul in the sheets until the fluttering stops. If you have been careful, this should involve hauling in only a few inches of sheet line.

On a beam reach the wind is ninety degrees to the course of the boat, or close to it. To set the sails for a beam reach, follow the procedure outlined above for the close reach. On many boats, this is the most exciting point of sailing. It is very fast, and if the rig is tuned properly, quite thrilling.

Your boat is on a broad reach when the wind is coming from aft of the beam but not from directly astern. Once again, the technique in setting the sails is to put the boat on course, ease out the sheets until the sails begin to luff, and then haul in the sheets until the luffing stops. If your boat has a masthead wind pennant, a good rule of thumb is to set the boom at an angle halfway between the line of the keel and the direction the wind pennant is pointing.

In a good breeze, with moderate seas running, a boat on a broad reach will surf down the front of waves as they pass under the boat. This is indeed exciting sailing.

RUNNING

A sailboat is running before the wind when the wind comes from astern or slightly on the quarter. To set the mainsail, the mainsheet is eased out until the boom is nearly at right angles to the centerline of the boat. If a boom vang is available, this is one time to use it, for the main should be as flat as possible. Without a vang, the boom will ride up and the mainsail will billow. Under these circumstances, the sail will chafe against the shrouds and spreader. This alters the sail's shape and may even result in a tear. The vang also serves to prevent an accidental jibe.

The working jib is useless on a run because it is blanketed by the mainsail. It is possible, however, to hold the jib out on the side opposite the main by a pole. The pole—called a *whisker pole*—extends from the clew of the jib to a point somewhere on the mast. A boat sailing this way is said to be sailing *wing-and-wing*.

As picturesque as sailing wing-and-wing is, it is not particularly fast, especially in very light winds. Clearly, since the principal driving force when running is the direct pressure of the wind on the sails, to increase

THE SKIPJACK

The skipjack oyster dredging fleet of Chesapeake Bay is the last remaining sail-driven working fleet in the United States. At one time more than one thousand of these interesting sailboats dotted the waters of Chesapeake Bay. Today some fifty make up the fleet, still operating because an 1865 Maryland conservation law requires the dredging of oysters by sail-driven vessels. During the early days of oyster dredging, skipjacks would dredge oysters until their holds were full and then race to the docks to obtain the best possible price, which usually went to the first catch in. Skipjacks are square sterned, beamy, and sharp prowed. Their shallow draft and centerboard enables them to work in shoal waters. The boats are usually rigged with a single mast raked aft, and a jib and leg-o-mutton mainsail. To honor these vessels, a last vestige of the great age of sail, an annual skipjack race is held on the Saturday nearest November 1, the opening of the oyster season. (Photo by Peter Barlow)

speed it is necessary to increase sail area. This is accomplished by flying a spinnaker. The spinnaker markedly increases the speed of a boat when running or broad reaching, for it offers much more sail area to the wind than a working jib. Indeed, you will sometimes see both a spinnaker and a working jib in use, with both sails drawing well.

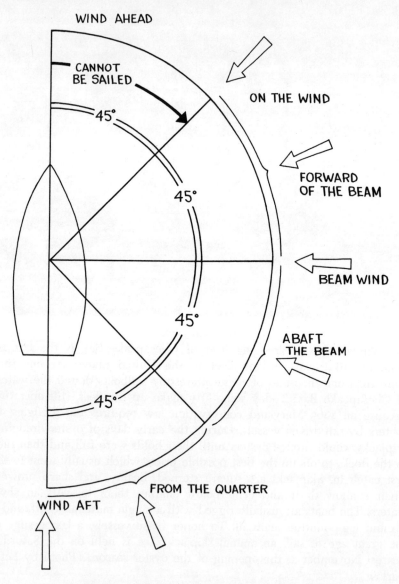

Relation of the wind to a boat under sail.

WIND AND A MOVING BOAT

Earlier in this chapter we mentioned *hauling* and *veering*. The wind is said to haul when it changes direction toward the bow of the boat. It is said to veer when it changes direction toward the stern. Both of these changes are in relation to the boat. That is, we are looking at wind change from the point of view of the boat.

It is also possible to view change in wind direction from the point of view of the horizon. Suppose the wind is coming from the north—we call this a north wind (wind is always named by the compass point from which it comes). Now, when the wind changes in an easterly direction (clockwise), it is said *to veer*. On the other hand, when it swings to westward (counterclockwise), it is said *to back*.

Additional new terminology is needed to describe how the wind comes in to a moving boat. It may, for example, strike the boat anywhere from dead ahead all the way to dead astern, either on the starboard or port side. The drawing gives these new terms. They are exactly the same on the opposite side of the boat.

When the wind is coming from within forty-five degrees of the heading of the boat, it is referred to as *wind ahead*. The forty-five-degree angle may vary. As we have pointed out, most boats will point up to about forty-five degrees to the wind. Some, however, sail closer than forty-five degrees, while many others do not even reach the forty-five-degree mark. When the wind is from the direction at which the boat points most efficiently, the term is *on the wind*.

Between the beating angle and almost directly abeam, the wind is *forward of the beam*. Then, when the wind is directly on the beam—a point ninety degrees from the heading of the boat—it is a *beam wind*. Wind arriving from a direction between ninety and 135 degrees from the bow is *wind abaft the beam*. *Wind from the quarter* is then wind coming in from 135 to 180 degrees from the heading of the boat. Finally, wind coming from directly behind the boat is called *wind astern*.

Pennants and *telltales*—pieces of cloth ribbon or yarn—attached to the masthead or shrouds indicate the direction of the wind on a boat. It's important to understand, however, that on a moving boat the pennant and telltales do not tell you the *true direction* of the wind. They tell you the direction of the *apparent wind*. Here's why. Look at the drawing. With the true wind on the beam, and the boat sailing forward, the pennant drags behind a bit because it is affected by the air the boat is moving through as well as by the beam wind. The result on the wind pennant is an angle slightly aft of the angle that would have been produced if the boat were standing still. Thus the position of the pennant on a moving boat makes the wind appear to be coming from a point farther ahead than it really is. This is the *apparent wind* direction. Many sailors refer frequently to the telltale while sailing because its position is an indication of the direction of the wind relative to the heading of the boat. Thus, as the diagram suggests, the telltale angle can help the skipper hold his course when the wind is constant, and it quickly reveals a wind shift when the wind is variable. A wind shift, of course, should be followed by an adjustment of the sail settings. The beginning sailor in particular will find keeping a close watch on the telltale a good habit to cultivate. In fact, actually sailing a boat in a large circle is a most instructive drill. Try it, and keep a close watch on the behavior of the telltale as the boat changes course relative to the wind.

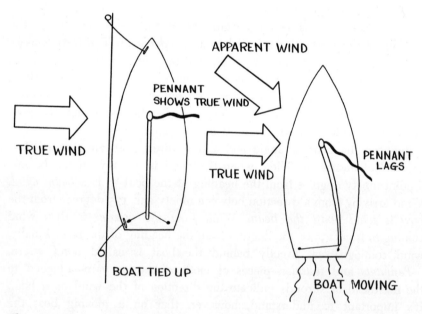

The apparent wind direction is slightly forward of the true wind direction. Apparent wind occurs because the pennant on a moving boat lags; it is affected by the air the boat is moving through as well as by the wind.

CORRECTING IMPROPER HELM

The way the wind interacts with a sailboat produces another important effect. This is the condition of "helm." A boat has helm if it spontaneously turns either into the wind or away from the wind when the tiller is released. If the boat turns into the wind, it is said to have *weather helm*. If it falls off, that is, turns away from the wind, it has *lee helm*. In both instances it is necessary to compensate with the rudder for the turning

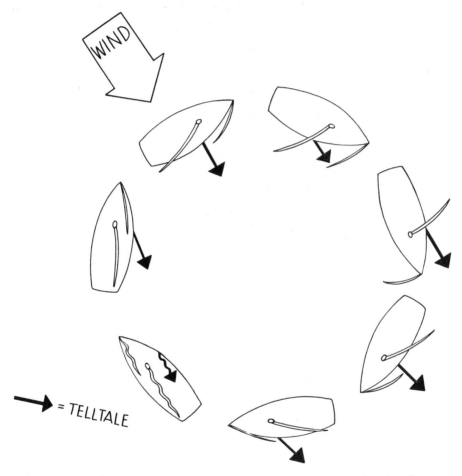

The telltale shows the direction of the wind relative to the heading of the boat. Many skippers use this convenient indicator to help them maintain course and to spot shifts in wind direction.

tendency. But this introduces drag because the rudder is turned while the boat is moving ahead. In the case of extreme helm, the resulting rudder drag can slow the boat down considerably.

A well-balanced boat should have very little helm. Many skippers, however, feel that a small amount of weather helm is desirable, for with it the boat tends to point up to its best position of beating. Lee helm, on the other hand, can be downright dangerous. It makes it difficult to head up into the wind when the boat had been hit by a sudden puff or squall, and could result in a capsize. As you will discover, the first thing to do in a sudden squall is head up into the wind and ease the sheets. Even more important, should a skipper sailing alone fall overboard, he would have no chance of getting back to a boat with a lee helm, for it would sail away from him.

Let's consider what causes improper helm and then point out how to correct it. As the drawing shows, a sailboat can be pictured as tending to turn on a vertical axis running down through the boat and center-

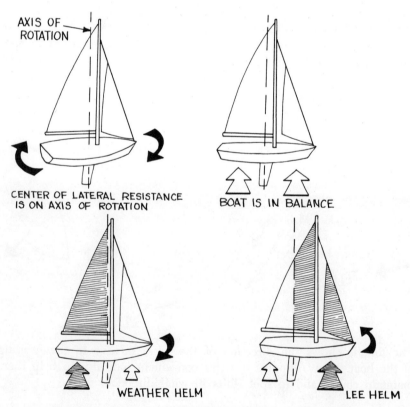

How adverse helm is produced. See text for details.

board. The *center of lateral resistance* of the boat—the point on the hull where a single force would exactly offset all of the side forces on the boat—lies on this axis. Now, if the wind pressure on the sails is exactly the same on either side of the center of lateral resistance, the boat is perfectly balanced; there will be no adverse helm. But if the wind pressure *aft* of the center of lateral resistance is the greater, weather helm results. In effect, the pressure difference drives the boat up into the wind. The reverse condition causes lee helm. The greater wind pressure *forward* of the center of lateral resistance drives the boat away from the wind.

There are several ways to correct adverse helm. Among these are (1) adjusting the jib and mainsail, (2) raising or lowering the centerboard, (3) shifting the weight of the crew or movable gear forward or aft, (4) changing the rake of the mast, and (5) moving the jibstay forward or aft. Of these corrective measures, the first three are carried out while under way. If adverse helm can't be satisfactorily corrected by these measures, permanent changes such as the latter two must be carried out.

Let's describe how to correct weather helm first, since this condition is the one you will most likely have to cope with. Keep in mind that weather helm occurs because there is greater wind pressure on the sails aft of the center of lateral resistance. *Easing the mainsheet* allows wind to spill from the main, thus reducing wind pressure. *Sheeting in the jib* has the effect of increasing wind pressure forward. Either or both of these measures will often greatly improve weather helm. Also try *raising the centerboard* a bit. This shifts the center of lateral resistance aft, but only reduces the area of centerboard in the water a slight amount. (This does not work with a daggerboard, for the only possible motion with a daggerboard is an up-and-down one.) Another way to move the center of lateral resistance aft is to *shift the crew or heavy weights* (such as anchor and the ice chest) *aft*. This lowers the stern in the water, and offers more lateral resistance aft than forward.

If these temporary measures fail to correct weather helm to your satisfaction, try the following more permanent adjustments. First, *decrease the rake of the mast,* that is, tip the mast forward a bit by easing up on the backstay and tightening up the jibstay. Don't forget to readjust the shrouds also. A very small change in the rake of the mast shifts a lot of sail area, so carry out this correction with care. On most boats you should not rake the mast forward of the vertical. Finally, you can try *moving the point of attachment of the jibstay forward* at the bow. This shifts sail area forward and reduces weather helm by a leverage effect. It works much the same as increasing the length of a crowbar increases the force that can be applied. In the case of the jib, sail area is moved forward, and greater wind leverage results forward of the center of lateral resistance.

Lee helm, which occurs because wind pressure forward of the center of lateral resistance is greater, is corrected by taking the opposite steps, that is, by moving the center of lateral resistance forward. While under way, try *hauling in the mainsheet* and *slacking the jibsheet*. Also *lower the centerboard* and *shift crew and movable weights forward*. Don't get the idea that you should do all of these things at once to correct adverse helm. As you come to know your boat, you will acquire a touch for just the right helm. Then, when the helm isn't quite correct, minor adjustment of one (and sometimes more) of the above controls will bring the helm back to where you want it. The more permanent adjustments for correcting lee helm, of course, are *raking the mast aft* and *moving the jibstay aft*. There are other permanent corrective measures for adverse helm, but they are beyond the scope of this book. If your boat does not respond to the suggestions given here, you should contact the boat's manufacturer for further suggestions.

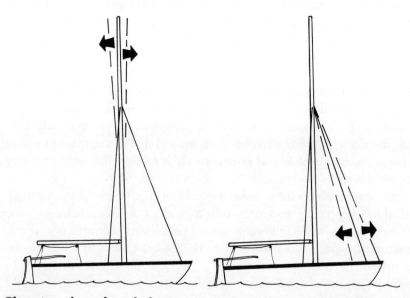

Changing the rake of the mast or the point of attachment of the jibstay will often be enough to correct an adverse helm. See text for details.

9. Preparing for a Sail

At last we are ready to get out on the water—in an imaginary way, of course. Many things, however, must be done before sailing away from a mooring or dock in a safe and seaworthy manner. It is important that you learn to perform all of these steps faithfully. Overlooking one or more may ruin your sailing fun by leading to a mishap of some sort. We will point out potential accidents as we go along.

To begin with, we assume that the boat is properly equipped with all of the required Coast Guard approved safety equipment, especially life jackets. In addition, there should be at least one paddle and a bucket or bilge pump aboard, plus an anchor and sufficient anchor line for the depth of water to be sailed on. If your boat is large enough, an outboard engine may be desirable. We can't emphasize too strongly the need for adequate safety equipment. Altogether too many boating accidents occur because the minimum required safety equipment was not on board.

To begin our first sail, we have to get out to the boat. This is no problem if it is tied up to a dock or in a slip, but may be one if it is necessary to row a dinghy out to a mooring. Don't overload the dinghy. An overloaded dinghy has very little freeboard, and is very unstable. Many a picnic lunch and many a bundle of dry gear (including clothing), plus two or three unhappy sailors, have wound up in the drink because a dinghy was overloaded. Make two trips or more if necessary.

Having gotten aboard the boat safely, several chores must be performed before bending on the sails. First, of course, the cockpit cover must be removed and stowed away. All loose gear on a sailboat should be carefully stowed away. The gear and rigging essential to sailing take up enough room without additional clutter. Next, lower the centerboard or daggerboard. This adds stability to the boat and prevents it from tipping too much as you move about. Now check the bilge for water. There may be either seepage (in the case of wood boats) or some accumulated rainwater. Pump out or sponge up any water; one mark of a good sailor is a dry boat. Finally, attach the tiller and rudder if this is necessary. On many smaller boats it is customary to store the tiller and rudder on the cockpit floorboards. Be careful when you climb aboard. Stepping down hard on a rudder or tiller can produce serious damage.

BENDING ON THE MAINSAIL

When a sloop is on a mooring and pointing into the wind, the rule is to raise the mainsail first. The general rule, in fact, is to raise the sails in a direction against the wind. Thus, when the bow points into the wind, the sails are raised going forward, the main first, the jib last. If the jib is raised first, the wind may cause the boat to turn and sail downwind. On the other hand, if the boat is pointed downwind, the jib is raised first. When we discuss leaving the mooring or dock the reasons for these rules will become clearer.

The sequence of steps for bending on and raising the mainsail are as follows. First, set the main in its sailbag beneath the *gooseneck fitting*—that is, beneath the point where the mast and boom come together. Unfasten the main halyard, make sure it is free aloft, and then attach it to the headboard of the sail. Do not, however, raise the sail at this point. Now draw the sail out of the bag, running your hand along the luff to make sure there are no snags or twists. Straighten out any twists before attempting to run the sail slides onto the track on the mast. After running all the slides on the track in the proper order, close the *slide stop* at the bottom of the track. This will keep the slides on the track and the sail in position along the luff for raising.

The next step is bending the foot of the sail on the boom. Begin by fastening the tack of the sail to the gooseneck fitting. Now run the entire foot of the sail through your hands to make sure it is straight and that no slides are twisted. Starting with the slide closest to the clew of the

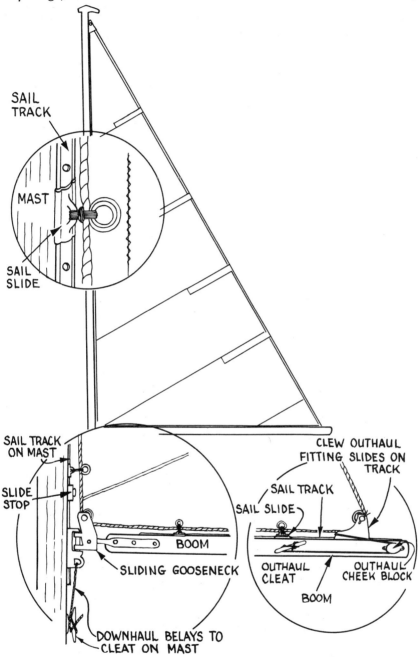

SAIL
TRACK

MAST

SAIL
SLIDE

SAIL TRACK
ON MAST

SLIDE
STOP

CLEW OUTHAUL
FITTING SLIDES ON
TRACK

SAIL TRACK

SAIL SLIDE

BOOM

SLIDING GOOSENECK

OUTHAUL
CLEAT

OUTHAUL
CHEEK BLOCK

BOOM

DOWNHAUL BELAYS TO
CLEAT ON MAST

Detail drawing of typical mainsail rigging at the gooseneck, the outhaul,
and along the sail track.

The spinnaker of this LS-16 sloop is set properly and drawing well. Note how carefully the skipper watches the spinnaker; even a small wind shift can collapse the spinnaker. (Photo by Chrysler Marine Products)

sail, thread the slides along the foot out onto the boom. The boom crutch should remain in place while this is being done. Now fasten the clew to the *outhaul fitting*. Pull the outhaul hand tight and cleat it. At this point, slide the battens into their sleeves along the leech of the sail, making sure that they are correctly fastened in place.

It's a good idea to mark the head, tack, and clew on your sails with indelible ink. Simply print the letters H, T, and C on the sailcloth near the corners of the sail. This will make it much easier for you to bend on sail directly from the sailbag. Do this for all of your sails, on both sides, but code the spinnaker on one side only. If you don't, you may find one of its corners twisted when you set the sail. Also, do not label the lower spinnaker corners T and C; P and S for port and starboard are better.

If your boat has a slotted mast and boom, there will be no sail slides. Instead, the bolt rope along the foot and luff of the sail is threaded into the slot, with the foot going on first. The one difference in the procedure is that you do not attach the luff of the sail to the mast before raising the sail. The bolt rope is threaded into the slot on the mast as the sail is raised. The simplest procedure is to have your crew feed the sail into the slot as you hoist the sail aloft.

The next step is raising the sail. Leave the boom crutch in position while the sail is being raised to prevent it from being stretched, but clear and slack the mainsheet. The sheet line should run through the proper fittings and be clear of the tiller and centerboard well. Tie a figure-eight knot in the end of the mainsheet to prevent it from running through the blocks. To put enough slack into the sheet, lift the boom overhead, and then replace it in the boom crutch. The last preparatory step to raising the main is releasing the downhaul. This will be tightened down to stretch the luff after the sail has been raised as far as it will go.

Hoist the sail, watching it carefully as you do. Make sure the slides are not twisted and that the battens are free of the spreader and shrouds as the sail goes up. The last one or two inches may be difficult, requiring a strong effort on your part. With the sail set up, lift the boom out of the crutch, stow the crutch in the cockpit, and allow the boom to fly. Watch out for your head!! Secure the halyard to its cleat, coil the line, and stow it in the bottom of the boat. Be sure to coil and stow the halyard so that it can be released instantly. The last step is adjusting the downhaul. Take up on the downhaul until the luff of the sail begins to wrinkle.

BENDING ON THE JIB

With the mainsail in position and properly adjusted, bend on and raise the jib. As the drawing shows, the sequence of the steps is as follows. First, place the jib in its bag on the foredeck, with the open end of the bag facing forward. Pull out the jib tack and shackle it to the deck fitting. Now draw the luff of the jib out of the bag and fasten the jib hooks to the jibstay. Start at the tack of the sail and work up, fastening the hooks in order. Make sure that the hooks all go on in the same direction and that the sail is not twisted. Free the jib halyard, make sure it is clear aloft, and fasten it to the head of the sail.

If your jib has battens, now is the time to put them in place. In any event, remove the remainder of the jib from the bag, stow the bag, and fasten the jibsheets to the clew of the sail. The sheet lines should be slack. Be sure the sheets are rigged correctly. On some boats they go outside the shrouds, on others inside the shrouds. Now raise the jib, keeping an eye on the sail as you do to make sure everything is in proper order. Take up the jib halyard so that the luff wire of the sail is taut. If the luff of the sail is loose and "scalloped," it will be far less efficient than when it is set up properly.

Be careful when you are handling halyards. On some boats, if you let the shackle go, the weight of the halyard will pull it up the mast. It may then jam in the sheave at the top of the mast. When this happens, it is almost impossible to shake the shackle loose. On small boats, you can beach the craft and tip it on its side to retrieve the halyard shackle. On larger boats, someone usually has to go up the mast, although it is occasionally possible to heel the boat close enough to a roof or bridge to recover the shackle. The best procedure is to be alert to the possibility of losing the shackle, and thus make sure it does not happen.

Well, there you are, the centerboard is down, the rudder and tiller are attached, and the sails have been hoisted. You're ready to cast off and sail away. Or are you? A moment's thought should tell you that although the boat may be ready to go, the skipper shouldn't be—not without a final check. First, check everything you did while making ready. Are the sails set properly? Is all the loose gear stowed away? Are the life jackets or Coast Guard approved safety cushions within easy reach? Is the paddle on board for use should the wind fail? Is the engine in operating condition? Is the rudder and tiller assembly functioning correctly? Are the sheet lines free and ready to use? Next, check the weather. Has the wind come up? Is a thunderstorm on its

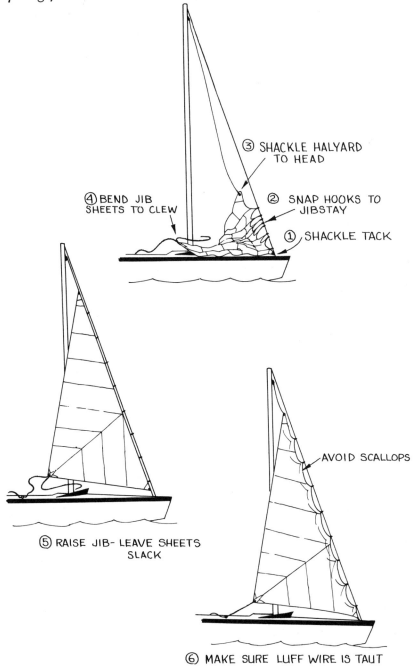

③ SHACKLE HALYARD TO HEAD

④ BEND JIB SHEETS TO CLEW

② SNAP HOOKS TO JIBSTAY

① SHACKLE TACK

⑤ RAISE JIB- LEAVE SHEETS SLACK

AVOID SCALLOPS

⑥ MAKE SURE LUFF WIRE IS TAUT

The sequence of steps for bending on the jib. For the sail to perform well, the luff wire must be tight.

way toward you? You would be surprised at the number of sailors who cast off in the face of a storm because they were so engrossed with raising the sails that they failed to check the weather.

LEAVING THE MOORING

We will consider two situations at a mooring: (1) the boat is pointing *into the wind* at the mooring, regardless of the strength and direction of the water current, and (2) the boat is pointing *downwind* at the mooring because the wind and current are opposite to each other, with the current stronger than the wind. Let's look at the first instance; it is the situation you will most frequently find yourself in.

You are ready to drop the mooring when the skipper is at the tiller and controls the mainsheet (which should still be slack), and the crew is forward ready to release the mooring buoy. The first step is to cast off (drop the buoy) and drift straight back to clear the mooring. Next, put the *jib aback* to turn the bow of the boat in the desired direction. With the bow turned, haul on the sheets to adjust the sails for a reach. Sail this way until the boat has picked up enough speed to adjust the sails for the desired course. Oh yes, you should have figured out where you wanted to go before leaving the mooring.

Let's take a closer look at the technique of putting the jib aback. This is a very easy maneuver for turning the bow of a boat when it is pointing into the wind. Make sure the jibsheets are loose and not cleated. Now grasp the clew of the jib and hold it out to the side opposite the direction the bow is to turn. If the boat has sternway, it will help to put the tiller over in the direction the bow is to swing. The wind will fill the jib and force the bow over. Just as soon as the boat has swung around to the point where a course can be sailed, let go the clew of the jib, put the tiller amidships, and haul the mainsheet and jibsheet so that the sails will fill and the boat will hold the desired course.

An altogether different technique is required to leave a mooring when the boat is pointing downwind. In this case the stern is pointing into the wind; thus the jib is raised first. Allow the jib to fly forward. Bend the mainsail to the mast and boom, but do not raise it while the boat is on the mooring. Leave the boom in its boom crutch. It is very difficult to hoist a mainsail downwind. In addition, once it fills with wind, it will drive the boat around wildly on the mooring. With the jib raised, drop

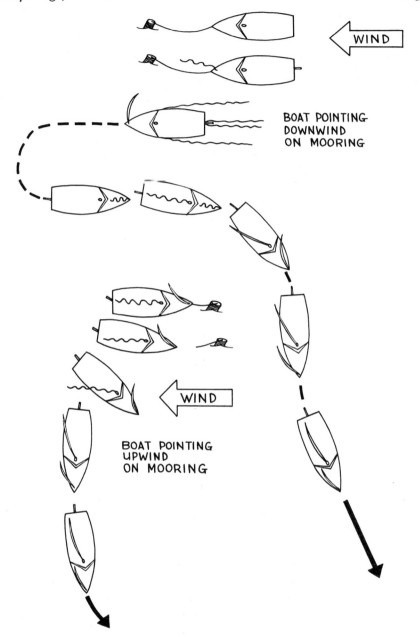

How to leave a mooring with the boat pointing downwind, as well as into the wind. Note that the jib is raised first when the boat is pointing downwind on a mooring.

the mooring buoy and haul the jibsheet until the sail fills. This will put you on a downwind tack under the jib alone. Sail on this tack until you are free of other boats and then round up into the wind. At this point, raise the mainsail as quickly as you can. Allow enough room, for the boat will drift some during the maneuver. Next, put the jib aback to turn the bow to your desired course, haul the sheets to a reaching position, and sail away. Finally, readjust the sails to the desired course once you have enough steerage way.

PUTTING JIB ABACK

How to put the jib aback to turn the bow of the boat. In this case, with the wind dead ahead, the crew is holding the jib to starboard in order to make the bow swing to port.

LEAVING A DOCK

Both leaving a dock and landing at a dock under sail are more difficult than the same maneuvers at a mooring. This is particularly true of landing at a dock, for it is difficult to judge a boat's momentum. Thus, very often a boat will either fetch up short of the dock or ram it with a resounding thump. At this point, however, we are still concerned with getting under way on our imaginary sail.

As the drawing shows, we will describe techniques for casting off a dock under four different wind conditions: (1) wind directly on the dock (a lee dock), (2) wind directly off the dock, (3) wind ahead of the boat, and (4) wind astern of the boat. One of these techniques will handle any wind direction other than those discussed. You will have to determine the one to use as you evaluate the wind. While we discuss what to do under each of these wind conditions, remember that you should try whenever possible to land at a dock with the boat headed into the wind. This makes getting away much easier.

Getting away from a lee dock may present a problem because the wind tends to hold the boat against the dock. If the wind is light enough, you may be able to paddle clear and then head up into the wind to raise the sails. It is also sometimes possible to sail away from a lee dock on the main alone. Have your crew push the bow away as you haul on the mainsheet. If the wind is not too strong, this should enable you to sail the boat clear before using the jib. If the wind is strong, you will have to *kedge out* from the dock before raising the sails. Using a dinghy, carry the anchor out fifty or seventy feet from the dock, and drop the anchor overboard. Your crew then hauls on the anchor line to pull the boat away from the dock. Once clear of the dock and other obstructions (it may take more than seventy feet), raise sails and up anchor, then sail away just as you would leave a mooring.

Casting off is quite simple when the wind is directly off a dock. Raise the jib only, and cast off the bowline first. Hauling the jibsheet will allow the sail to fill and swing the bow out. With the boat pointing downwind, cast off the stern line and sail downwind on the jib alone. Once the boat is clear of all obstacles, round up into the wind to raise the main. From this point on, the technique is the same as leaving a mooring downwind.

The most desirable wind condition for getting away from a dock is wind dead ahead of the boat. Both main and jib can be raised;

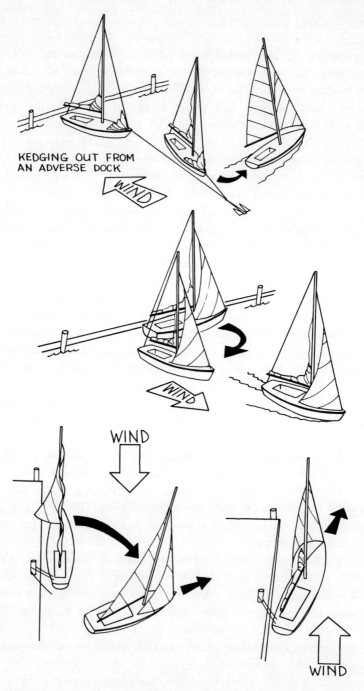

KEDGING OUT FROM
AN ADVERSE DOCK

WIND

WIND

WIND

WIND

Leaving a dock under sail with the wind from several different directions.

the boat can then be sailed clear by putting the jib aback, pushing the bow out with a boathook, and hauling sheets to leave the dock on a reach. It will help to use a stern line or *spring line* (see Chapter 12) to hold the stern in place while the bow swings out. Be sure the line is fastened to the cleat or pile so that it can be released instantly from the boat.

Another difficult situation is wind dead astern, or nearly so. As in the case of wind directly off the dock, it will be necessary in this instance to sail away from the dock on the jib alone. The main is not to be raised until the boat has been sailed clear and up into the wind. Again using a stern line or spring line, push the bow away from the dock using a boathook, and haul on the jibsheet until the jib fills and begins to draw the boat away from the dock. Drop the stern line, and sail free on the jib alone. Once you are clear of other obstructions, head up into the wind and raise the main.

Well, it took a bit of doing, but we are finally "under way." The weather is fine, the wind is just right, the sails are set properly, and all safety gear is aboard and within reach. We are free to sail where we please. But as you will see, there is a bit more to it than just pointing the boat in the direction we want to sail. In the next chapter we tackle the problem of "getting there from here" in a sailboat.

10. Under Way!

Let's assume that we have successfully navigated clear of all other boats, and that we are on open water. This means that we have probably sailed through an anchorage, or perhaps out through a channel. At the moment, we are interested in sailing techniques on open water. Later we will discuss the rules that govern the movement of boats in channels and anchorages, and under congested conditions.

Regardless of whether you are out sailing simply for the pleasure of it, with no particular destination in mind, or you are sailing to a particular point, it is necessary to know how to sail a boat in all directions. As indicated earlier, you can't always point the boat in the desired direction and sail away. For example, you already know that it is impossible to sail directly into the wind. How then does the sailor take his boat to a destination that lies directly upwind?

TACKING

To take a boat to a point directly upwind, it is necessary to sail a zigzag course. This is called *beating*. Each leg of the zigzag course is sailed as closehauled as possible, with an angle of about ninety degrees between courses. As the drawing shows, this ninety-degree angle between tacks results because the boat sails closehauled at about forty-five degrees to the wind.

There are two ways to tack to a point directly upwind. Frequent short tacks or fewer long tacks may be made. The choice between short and long tacks is a matter of judgment. You will have to evaluate each situation you find yourself in and then act accordingly. Experience helps a great deal, as you will discover when you have been sailing for a while. We might make one suggestion, however. If you are not familiar with navigating by compass and chart, it is wise not to lose sight of your point or marker—that is, the place you are trying to reach. This marker may be a buoy, a flagpole, or a house of a particular color on shore. By taking a series of short tacks, you can usually keep this marker in sight. On the other hand, if you take a long tack, you may sail out of sight of the marker. You may even sail far above it and lose time as a result.

Now, suppose you are on the last tack. How do you judge when to come about so that the boat will sail directly to the marker? The answer is quite simple. If the boat is capable of sailing at forty-five degrees to the wind, you wait until the mark is exactly on the beam—

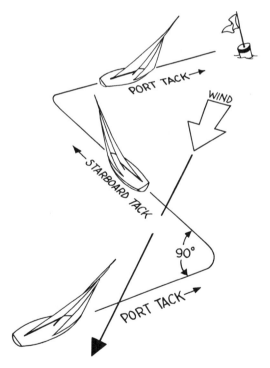

Tacking is sailing a zigzag course upwind. It is a necessary tactic to reach a destination that lies in the windward direction.

that is, at ninety degrees to the course of the boat. This is easy to judge. Face forward and extend your arm at right angles to the course of the boat on the side of the marker. Sight along your arm. When it points directly at your destination, continue on course for a bit to allow for leeway, and then come about. Of course, if your boat does not point as close as forty-five degrees to the wind, an angle greater than ninety degrees will be necessary.

As the drawing indicates, if your destination is directly upwind, the tacks needed to get there will be of equal length. Very frequently, however, you will find your marker off to the left of upwind or

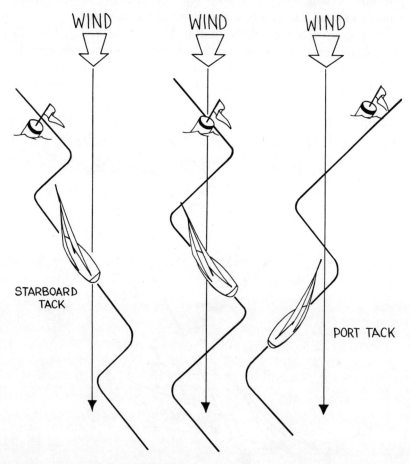

As the wind shifts away from a marker on either side, it becomes possible to alternate long tacks with short tacks. When the wind is coming directly from the marker, the tacks may be equal in length.

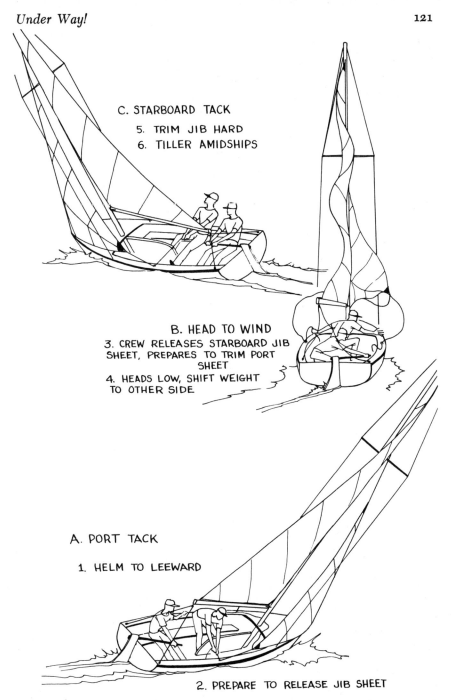

C. STARBOARD TACK
  5. TRIM JIB HARD
  6. TILLER AMIDSHIPS

B. HEAD TO WIND
3. CREW RELEASES STARBOARD JIB
SHEET, PREPARES TO TRIM PORT
SHEET
4. HEADS LOW, SHIFT WEIGHT
TO OTHER SIDE

A. PORT TACK

1. HELM TO LEEWARD

2. PREPARE TO RELEASE JIB SHEET

The sequences of steps during "coming about." Good coordination is required to come about smoothly.

off to the right of upwind. Under these circumstances, you will want to alternate long and short tacks. If the wind is coming from a point to the right of your destination, the long tack will be a starboard tack. Just the opposite occurs if the wind is coming from a point to the left of your marker. In this case, the long tack is the port tack. Try to visualize what happens when the marker is farther away from the wind direction on one side or the other. Do you see that this means the long tack will be longer, and the short tack shorter? Eventually, of course, it becomes possible to reach the target on just one long tack.

Up to this point, we have spoken of tacking without paying any attention to the technique of turning a sailboat so that the wind is changed from one side to the other. There are two ways to do this: *coming about* and *jibing*. Let's look at coming about first.

COMING ABOUT

When a boat comes about, it has changed from one tack to the other, with the bow swinging through the eye of the wind.

If you study the drawing, you will get a clear picture of the events that take place during the coming-about maneuver. Let's assume, for

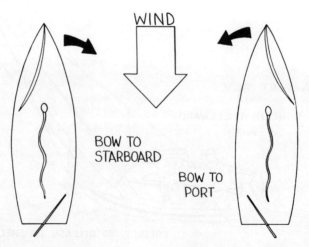

When caught "in irons," put the jib aback to turn the boat so that the sails will catch the wind.

example, that we are sailing closehauled on the port tack, and it is decided to come about. The helmsman first gives the command, "Ready about!" This alerts the crew to be ready to handle sheet lines and move to the other side of the boat. A few moments later, after the crew has indicated that they are ready, the helmsman gives the command "Hard-a-lee!" to actually begin the maneuver.

Several events then take place at the same time. First, the helmsman puts the tiller over to leeward, causing the bow to swing into the wind. Just as soon as the jib starts to luff, the jibsheet is released by the crew. The bow then swings through the eye of the wind, with the sails luffing, and falls off with the wind on the other side. The mainsail fills with the wind, but the jibsheet has to be hauled to trim the jib for the new course. During these maneuvers, the crew has been moving across the boat to the other side. The crew members time their movement as the boat turns so that they arrive to windward just as the sails fill and the boat moves off on its new course. Finally, the tiller is put amidships, and the boat is steered to its new course.

If the boat is closehauled before coming about, and the skipper intends to sail closehauled on the new tack, the mainsheet is left alone. The sail will fill properly on the opposite tack. Frequently, however, a boat is brought about from a reach. In this instance, as the boat is headed up into the wind, it is necessary to haul on both the mainsheet and the jibsheet so that drive is maintained in the sails. Then, after the turn has been accomplished, the mainsail and the jib must be adjusted for the new course.

Sometimes a boat will fail to come about, and end up bow into the wind with the sails luffing. This can occur for a variety of reasons. The boat may have had insufficient way on, or the crew's weight may have been poorly distributed. The helmsman may not have brought the boat around smartly enough, or the crew may have released the jib too soon. Also, the helmsman may have jammed the tiller over too rapidly, causing the rudder to act as a brake. In any event, when this happens the boat is said to be "*in irons.*" It refuses to answer to the helm, and drifts backward helplessly. Eventually, as it drifts back, the boat will fall off one way or the other, and the sails will fill. There is no way of knowing, however, whether it will fall off on the tack the skipper wants.

Of course, it is best to avoid getting into irons, but should it happen, correction is fairly simple. The trick is to put the jib aback so that the bow will fall off in the desired direction. To make the bow go to starboard and put the boat on the port tack, back the jib to port and put

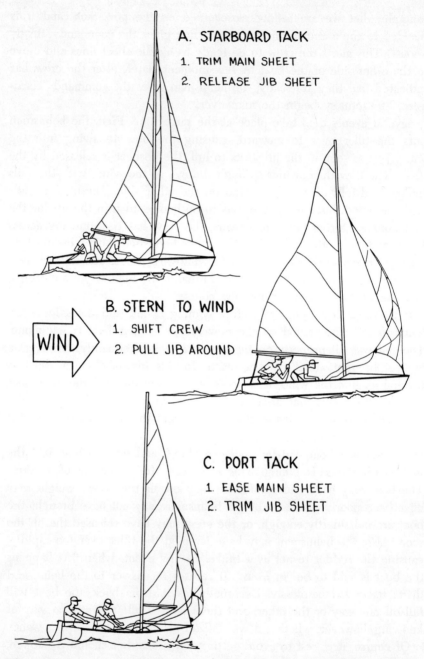

A. STARBOARD TACK

1. TRIM MAIN SHEET
2. RELEASE JIB SHEET

B. STERN TO WIND

1. SHIFT CREW
2. PULL JIB AROUND

WIND

C. PORT TACK

1. EASE MAIN SHEET
2. TRIM JIB SHEET

The sequence of steps during "jibing." A boat should be jibed in light to moderate winds only. In heavy winds jibing is a dangerous maneuver.

the tiller to starboard. Just the opposite is done to make the bow fall off to port. As the boat falls off, wait until it is fully about before setting the tiller for the new course and trimming the sheets.

If you are sailing a boat with no jib, the technique is the same except that the mainsail is backed. Wait until the boat begins to drift backward, then back the main and put the rudder over on the same side as the backed main.

JIBING

When a sailboat jibes, the boat is brought around to the opposite tack by putting the stern through the eye of the wind. In effect, jibing is the opposite of coming about. A boat is usually jibed when sailing before the wind and a course change is desired, but the skipper wants to avoid coming about. Sometimes when sailing downwind, the wind will shift so that it is coming from the same side of the boat the boom is on. This is called sailing *by the lee.* It is a dangerous condition, for the wind may get behind the main and produce an accidental jibe. As mentioned earlier, the rapidly swinging boom during an accidental jibe can be very dangerous to the crew and rigging.

The jibe should not be attempted in strong winds by beginning sailors. Not only is the flying boom a hazard to the crew, there is also the possibility that its momentum will tear out the shrouds and stays and dismast the boat. It is much safer to sheet in the sails, come about, and then ease off to the new course.

The jibe is easy to perform in light and moderate winds. Here's how it is done. Assume the boat is on a broad reach with the boom eased well out from the boat. Make sure the centerboard is fully lowered to add stability. To begin the jibe, haul in the mainsheet to bring the boom in toward the centerline of the boat. Hold course while bringing in the boom. Release the jibsheet at this point, and immediately change course. The boom will swing over to the other side of the boat as the wind gets behind it. Shift the crew to the other side of the boat at this time. Next, quickly ease out the mainsheet until the sail is in position for the new course. Trim the jibsheet to set the jib in its new position on the opposite side of the boat.

Special precautions must be followed when handling sheets during a jibe. The sheets should never be fastened, but rather hauled and held by hand. In addition, the sheets must be kept clear so that they can be run out after jibing without snarling.

Sometimes, when a boat is sailing downwind, the wind will repeatedly shift a few degrees back and forth. This makes it difficult to sail without jibing. But if the wind is strong and the seas rough, the wise skipper won't want to jibe. The preferred tactic is to *tack downwind*. In tacking downwind, a zigzag course downwind is followed. The boat is sailed on a broad reach. When the opposite tack is desired, the boat is brought all the way around and up into the wind; it comes about and then falls off to a broad reach. Coming about is always safer than jibing. Moreover, when tacking downwind the boat is sailing on a broad reach, which is safer than running with the wind directly astern. When the wind is directly astern, there is always the possibility of an accidental jibe.

When a boat is under control, heavy weather sailing can be very exciting. The good sailor, however, learns to judge the weather in terms of his boat's capabilities, and stays in port when conditions are too rough. (Photo by Peter Barlow)

THE SPINNAKER

Since the spinnaker is never raised on a mooring or at a dock, but rather when a boat on open water turns onto a downwind course, this seems a good point in our imaginary cruise to describe how it is handled. No sail is as exciting in use as the spinnaker, which adds drive to a boat on all points of sailing from a beam reach to running before the wind. The spinnaker is so powerful a sail it is useless to race without one against a boat that has one. Despite its great beauty and power, however, the spinnaker is very difficult to handle correctly. To be good at working with one, a crew must practice long and hard. Many a race has been lost because the crew was inept with the spinnaker. There are two or three different ways to set a spinnaker flying. For the sake of simplicity, we will describe the method most widely used on small boats. Let's assume that the boat is sailing on a broad reach, and that the skipper has given the order to raise the spinnaker. The sail is brought forward in its sail bag, or in a "turtle." Prior to leaving home port, the sail had been carefully folded and stored with its three corners sticking out at the top. The bag or turtle is placed on the outside of the jibstay and lashed in place.

The halyard is attached to the head of the sail first. Make sure it is free of the stays and shrouds, for the spinnaker must be set above the jibstay. Next, attach the guy and sheet lines. The guy is led aft outside the windward shrouds, and the sheet is brought aft outside the leeward shrouds. The spinnaker pole is rigged next. It is attached at its base to the mast-tack slide and brought forward so that its end is just above the spinnaker bag on the windward side. The forward end of the pole is snapped to the guy line at this point. The spinnaker is now properly rigged and ready to set. It never hurts, though, to take one last look to make sure something hasn't been overlooked.

The procedure for setting the sail is as follows. First, the sail is raised by the halyard, which is then cleated down. Next, the after guy line is hauled in until the spinnaker pole is approximately parallel to the boom—that is, at right angles to the apparent wind. The pole should also be parallel to the horizon. This is done by adjusting the pole topping lift and foreguy. Finally, the sheet line is eased until the luff of the sail is just full and curling. Having set the spinnaker, the jib may be dropped. During this procedure, the skipper controls the after guy line and sheet line, while the crew handles the spinnaker halyard and adjusts the position of the pole. With the sail set, the crew takes over the guy and sheet lines, and the skipper gives his full attention to the tiller.

Trimming the spinnaker while under way is a demanding job. It requires perfect coordination between skipper and crew at all times. With the boat on the desired course, the crew must adjust the sail to every shift of the wind. This means watching the luff of the sail and adjusting the sheet line to keep the luff full but on the edge of a curl, as well as keeping the spinnaker pole at right angles to the apparent wind.

Clearly, with the spinnaker flying, it is impossible to come about. Often, however, it is necessary to change course so that the wind comes in to the boat from the opposite side. To do this, it is necessary to *jibe*

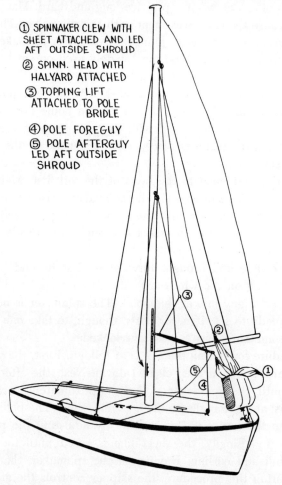

① SPINNAKER CLEW WITH SHEET ATTACHED AND LED AFT OUTSIDE SHROUD
② SPINN. HEAD WITH HALYARD ATTACHED
③ TOPPING LIFT ATTACHED TO POLE BRIDLE
④ POLE FOREGUY
⑤ POLE AFTERGUY LED AFT OUTSIDE SHROUD

Set up for raising the spinnaker. See the text for details. Double check all rigging before actually raising the spinnaker.

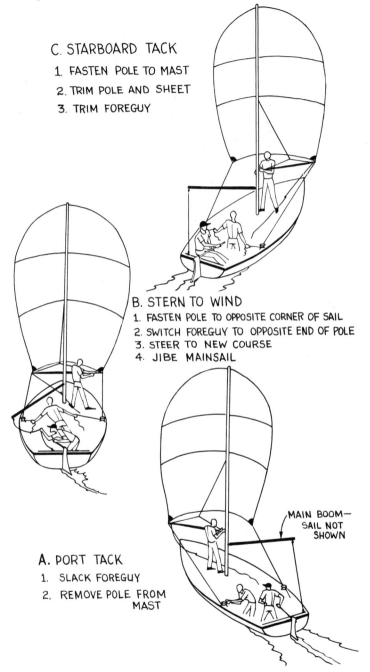

C. STARBOARD TACK
1. FASTEN POLE TO MAST
2. TRIM POLE AND SHEET
3. TRIM FOREGUY

B. STERN TO WIND
1. FASTEN POLE TO OPPOSITE CORNER OF SAIL
2. SWITCH FOREGUY TO OPPOSITE END OF POLE
3. STEER TO NEW COURSE
4. JIBE MAINSAIL

MAIN BOOM—
SAIL NOT
SHOWN

A. PORT TACK
1. SLACK FOREGUY
2. REMOVE POLE FROM
      MAST

The sequence of steps in "jibing the spinnaker." The mainsail has been left out for the sake of clarity.

the spinnaker. In essence, jibing the spinnaker amounts to shifting the spinnaker pole from one side of the boat to the other at the moment the boat's course is changed and the mainsail is jibed. The sequence of steps is shown in the drawing.

The first step is to slack the foreguy to allow the spinnaker pole to be shifted. The crew forward then removes the pole from its fitting on the mast and attaches the pole end to the other corner of the sail. Next, the foreguy is shifted to the opposite corner of the sail. At this point, the skipper steers the boat to its new course, and jibes the mainsail. While this is taking place, the crew releases the spinnaker pole from the original corner it was attached to, and fastens that end of the pole to the mast-track slide.

This completes the jibe, except for trimming the sheet and resetting the pole at right angles to the apparent wind. Note that the "old" sheet line is now the after guy line, and that the "old" after guy line is now the sheet line.

Getting the spinnaker up, trimming it properly, and mastering the jibe does not complete the story. It's also necessary to know how to get the sail down without getting into trouble. Sloppy spinnaker work can result in an unbelievable mess, and possibly a torn sail; it takes care and speed to avoid this kind of snarl-up. The first thing to do is raise the jib. Next, the after guy is slacked to swing the pole forward against the jibstay. This allows the spinnaker to swing around behind the mainsail, where it will be blanketed and collapse. The pole is now unsnapped from the mast, and the sheet line hauled in so that the clew of the sail is in the crew's hands. As one member of the crew lowers the halyard, the sail is hauled into the cockpit under the foot of the main. The halyard should not be dropped so fast that the sail droops into the water. If the spinnaker is pulled under the boat, you are in big trouble, for it is very difficult to get the sail back on board.

As the spinnaker is taken in, it should be stuffed into its bag with the sheet, guy, and halyard attached. Start at the bottom, stowing the sail so that it will come out the next time ready to fly.

11. Sailing in Heavy Weather

Sooner or later every sailor, despite the routine precaution of checking the weather before going out, finds himself sailing in rough weather. Obviously, there are certain dangers associated with sailing under rough conditions. How such experiences turn out depends entirely upon three factors: (1) how well the sailor understands the various wind and sea conditions he can expect to meet, (2) how well he prepares himself, his crew, and his craft for heavy going, and (3) the physical limitations of his sailboat. All three are important. The sturdiest sailboat is useless in a blow if the skipper fails to take measures to make it seaworthy. Let's assume now that we have run into some rough going on our imaginary sail, and discuss what to do about it.

WIND AND WAVE CONDITIONS

In general, waves are produced by wind. Over the ocean, strong storm winds build up the long waves commonly referred to as "swell." In addition to these, local winds produce the choppy conditions you are most likely to encounter as a small-boat sailor. The important point to remember is that strong winds produce potentially dangerous waves. Sometimes these conditions come up very suddenly. The alert skipper must be ready to cope with them when they occur.

Both strong winds and the waves they generate pose hazards to the small-boat sailor. Let's look at the types of wind and wave conditions you can expect to meet, and then describe how they can be handled. With respect to wind, you can look for strong, steady winds, or strong, puffy winds. Strong, steady winds occur in large storms, but they also may occur during the clear weather that follows the passage of a cold front. These winds can usually be predicted in advance; thus you should be able to avoid them.

Strong, puffy winds are more hazardous, as well as more difficult to predict. These winds occur in the thunderstorms and in the sudden squalls that sailors run into so often during the passage of weather fronts. It is the changeability of puffy winds that causes difficulty. They vary from extremely strong to light, and change direction rapidly. Thus, if the skipper is not alert, he may be caught in an accidental jibe or be capsized by a sudden puff from a different direction.

On sheltered waters, such as harbors and small lakes, the long waves of the open ocean are not present. In high winds, however, steep, choppy waves often develop. These waves are particularly troublesome because they can come from many different directions. It is very difficult to judge where the next wave will come from; thus the skipper must always be on the lookout.

WHAT TO DO IN A SUDDEN SQUALL

Head up into the wind.

Release main and jib sheets.

Haul sails down at once.

Drop centerboard all the way.

Put on life jackets.

How do you judge when the wind is too strong for sailing? This depends on the size and sturdiness of your boat, plus your ability as a sailor. A reliable indicator, however, is the presence of whitecaps. The beginner in a small boat should consider staying in port or coming in at once if the water is covered with whitecaps.

For more experienced sailors, it is possible to sail under more strenuous conditions. In fact, some of the most exciting sailing is done in good, stiff breezes. When the wind is blowing at eleven to sixteen knots, whitecaps first appear. This is a "moderate breeze" on the Beaufort Wind

THE SNEAK BOX

Introduced on Barnegat Bay, New Jersey, in the late 1830s, the sneak
box was originally used primarily for hunting and fishing. The name
"sneak box" came into being because the boats could be very quietly
rowed or pushed close to the game. Early sneak boxes were twelve
to fourteen feet long with a 4½-to-5-foot beam. Later on the boats
were built with lengths up to twenty feet. These later variations were
used for sailing and racing. Some were gaff-rigged, as the boat shown
here, and some had jib-headed rigs. During the 1920s a large class of
fifteen-footers raced regularly on Barnegat Bay. Growing interest in
other types of boat at that time, however, led to the decline of sneak
boxes. (Photo by Peter Barlow)

Scale. For boats under twelve feet in length, sailing is potentially hazardous in a moderate breeze.

In a "fresh breeze" (seventeen to twenty-one knots) the length of the waves has increased, and whitecaps cover the water. Gusts, however, are often considerably stronger than twenty-one knots. Sailing under these conditions is usually safe for skillful sailors in boats sixteen to twenty feet in length, but the going is rough and wet. Small boats should not be out in winds in excess of twenty-one knots, for the danger may be too great.

REEFING

The wind is up, and the going is rough. We elect to adjust by reducing the sail area exposed to the wind. With shortened sails, sailing in high winds is considerably safer because both speed and angle of heel decrease. The boat is thus a lot easier to handle. There are two ways to shorten sail. One of these is to use sails with a smaller surface area. The *storm jib* was mentioned in Chapter 5. In addition, many skippers carry smaller mainsails for use in windy weather. The second way to reduce sail area is *reefing*. This is simply a technique for furling or rolling up a portion of the sail in use.

Many newer boats have *roller reefing* for both the mainsail and jib. For the mainsail, the boom is specially rigged at the gooseneck and the sheet attachment so that it can be rolled like a window shade. To reef the main, the sail is luffed and then lowered gradually while the crew rolls it up on the boom. As this is being done, the sail must be pulled out toward the clew to smooth out wrinkles and prevent folding or bunching. A mainsail rigged for roller reefing is quite convenient, for it eliminates the need to change sails. Roller reefing is also easier than tying in reef points, the older method for reefing the main.

More and more boats today are being equipped with roller reefing jibs. These rigs solve two problems. They permit the skipper to shorten sail on the jib without leaving the cockpit, and they provide a neat and simple way to furl and store the jib. In operation, the roller reefing jib winds up on the jibstay when the sail is shortened. The jib is then unfurled by drawing on the sheet line after releasing the furling line.

In the older, more conventional method of reefing the mainsail, one or more lines of reef points are sewn into the sail parallel to the boom. Reef points are small cords sewn into patches set into the sail. Large

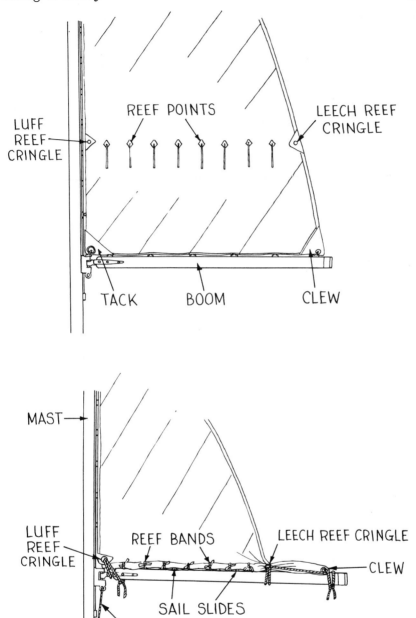

How a reef is tied into a sail. Note that the reef points are tied around the sail only, not around the boom.

brass rings, called *cringles,* are set into the sail at either end of the line of reef points. The forward cringle is the *luff cringle,* the after one is the *leech cringle.*

Not all sailboats have reef points in their sails. Enough do, however, to make a description of their use worthwhile. Try to remember that if it is necessary to reef, it is a lot easier to do it before going out. Reefing while out in rough weather can be a difficult and potentially hazardous task.

The steps in reefing the main are as follows. Since we are already out on the water, first luff the main. Next, lower the mainsail partially, and draw the sail up to the boom along the line of reef points. Lash the luff cringle to the boom as shown in the drawing, and follow by lashing the leech cringle to the outhaul and around the boom. Now pull out and flatten the fold of sail formed by tying down the cringles.

Furl (roll up) the folded-off portion of the sail into a tight cylinder. With the furled sail in place, start at the luff and tie reef points around it. Use a square knot and tie the reef points around the sail only, *not* around the boom. If your sail is equipped with grommets without reef

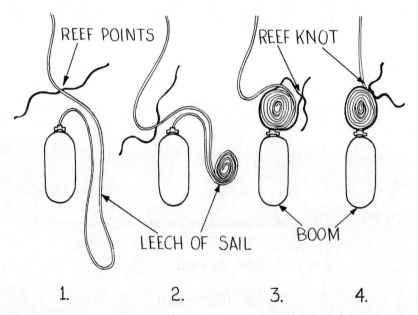

Cross section from astern of a boom and sail during the reefing process. If the folded-off portion of the sail is rolled up carefully, the reef will be compact and neat.

points, start at the forward end of the sail and pass a lacing around the furled sail, but not around the boom. Tie the lacing at the clew.

Avoid leaving a reef in a sail any longer than is necessary, for it can distort the shape of the sail. Shaking out a reef is quite simple. Just reverse the steps in tying in the reef. Untie the reef points, release the outhaul and luff lashings, and then raise the sail all the way. Take care to be sure all lashings and reef points have been released before raising the sail.

HEAVY WEATHER SAILING TACTICS

In addition to reefing, several sailing tactics will help us stay under control in the strong winds we have encountered. Before discussing these tactics, however, we want to emphasize again what to do when your boat is hit by a sudden and very strong puff of wind. First, *head up into the wind* to take the puff head on. Second, *release the sheet lines* to spill the wind out of the sails. In practice, you will learn to release the

---

WHAT TO DO IN HEAVY WEATHER SAILING

Put on warm and waterproof clothing.

Stay near shore where water is smoother.

Reef sail if wind becomes too strong.

Keep boat as level as possible.

Flatten main by tightening outhaul and downhaul.

Do not tie sheet lines down; make sure halyards can be released at a moment's notice.

Head up in strong puffs.

Avoid unnecessary tacking.

Avoid jibes.

Put on life jackets.

sheets just as the boat acquires enough momentum to carry the bow up into the wind.

If the wind should become too strong for reefed sails or jib alone, we can drop the mainsail first and then the jib, and then run before the wind under bare poles. If speed becomes excessive, the boat may broach or take heavy seas from astern. To slow the boat down trail a long line, a bucket, or a sea anchor over the stern.

If it is necessary to go to windward with full sail in strong winds, try sailing on a tight jib and a luffing mainsail. This tactic is called the

FISHERMAN'S REEF

A tight jib that backwinds the main, along with a luffing main, is called the "fisherman's reef." It is one way to handle high winds when beating.

"fisherman's reef." With the main eased out and luffing, the sail's drive is sharply reduced. At the same time, however, it still has some drive in the leech. In addition, the jib will backwind the main, also cutting down on the drive of the sails. With less drive, the boat will sail in a more erect position, and also sail slower. In heavy weather it is necessary to reduce speed to minimize slamming into head seas. While sailing under a fisherman's reef, remember to hold the main and jibsheets by hand, with only a turn of the line around a cleat or winch. You must be ready to release the sheets at once if the wind becomes too strong.

The safest point of sailing in strong winds is *broad reaching*. This is true partly because the boat is erect when broad reaching, and partly because the skipper can play the sails against the wind. In strong puffs, the sheets are eased out and the boat is luffed up. On the other hand, when the wind softens, the sheets are hauled and the boat may be returned to its course. Both the main and the jib should be eased out until they luff, with just the after portions of the sails supplying drive. Sailed this way, broad reaching under rough going allows a maximum of control over varying wind conditions.

If the wind is too strong for reefing or one of the other tactics for sailing under full sail, it is possible to sail under either the mainsail or the jib alone. If your desired course will permit you to sail on a reach, you will have more control of the boat under main alone than under jib alone. You can play the varying strength of the wind as in broad reaching. In addition, because the sail area is concentrated aft of the center of lateral resistance, the boat will have a strong weather helm, and thus head up into the wind quite easily.

If it is possible for you to run before the wind, sailing under the jib

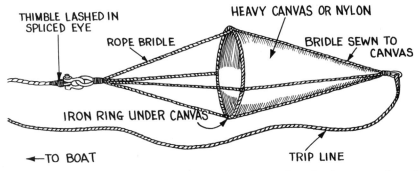

A typical sea anchor. The trip line spills the anchor to vary speed and also to haul the anchor back aboard.

alone is relatively safe in strong winds. If your boat is not equipped with a storm jib, the working jib alone provides the smallest possible amount of sail area. Running or broad reaching under jib alone is steady and fairly easy to manage. It is much more difficult to control the course of the boat when beam reaching or going to windward on jib alone, for the boat will make more leeway than usual. In addition, the helmsman will be working with a lee helm, which, as we have pointed out, is undesirable.

If the wind becomes so strong that running with jib alone or under bare poles is dangerous, that is, if the boat threatens to turn broadside to the waves and be swamped, it will be necessary to trail some sort of *sea anchor* over the stern. This will slow the boat down and will probably hold the stern to the waves. Various types of sea anchors are available. One is shown in the drawing. The speed of a boat running with a sea anchor out is controlled by the trip line of the anchor. By pulling on the trip line, the anchor is spilled and the boat moves faster. As mentioned earlier, dragging anything over the stern, from a long line to a swamped dinghy, serves as a sea anchor. Let's hope that you are never in the unfortunate position of requiring a sea anchor. In general, careful attention to the weather before going out can prevent such mishaps.

WHAT TO DO TO
PREVENT A CAPSIZE

Head boat up into wind.

Release all sheet lines, and lower centerboard all the way.

Lower and tie down sails.

Secure boom tightly in boom crutch; tighten jib sheets.

Secure all loose gear.

Put on life jackets.

Sit on floor of cockpit.

Anchor if possible.

If you must run, drag a sea anchor.

WHAT TO DO WHEN CAPSIZED

The commonest reaction to a capsize, especially from beginners, is surprise. They all say they had no idea it was about to happen. Centerboard boats capsize for a variety of reasons (keel boats rarely capsize). A sudden puff of wind too strong for the sail area carried, too little speed, failure to rebalance crew weight while coming about, and jibing in a strong wind with the centerboard up are just a few. In the case of beginning sailors, inexperience and misjudgment of wind and sea conditions are also important factors.

We can't emphasize too strongly the importance of preventing a capsize. The box summarizes what you should do to minimize the chances of capsizing. Read its contents carefully. In a nautical paraphrase of Smokey the Bear, "Only *you* can prevent a capsize." Unfortunately, capsizing can be as great a disaster as a forest fire in terms of loss of life. Very few people seem to know the correct things to do after they have been dumped into the water.

The most important rule is "STAY WITH THE BOAT." Obviously,

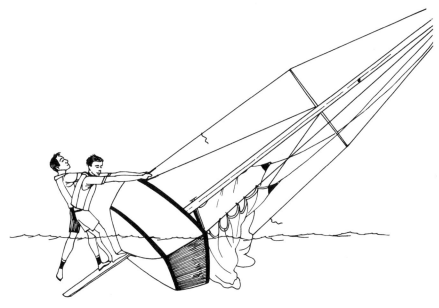

With the sails removed and lashed down, it is often possible to right a capsized centerboard boat by standing on the centerboard and applying leverage. Always stay with a capsized boat if it will support the crew.

this refers to a boat that will support the entire crew when it is swamped. A recent tragedy on Lake Michigan illustrates just how important this rule is. Two boys and a girl capsized in a small sailboat within view of about twenty people on shore. A rescue operation was started at once, but the only boat available had a balky engine that would not start. In the fifteen minutes it took to start the engine, both boys had drowned. They had started swimming for shore thinking that it was only a couple of hundred yards away. Both boys were excellent swimmers, but that "couple of hundred yards" turned out to be something over a mile. When the girl was finally picked up, she reported that one of the boys had called the other "chicken" because he had wanted to stay with the boat rather than strike out for shore.

Again and again lives are lost because people leave capsized boats. They don't realize that most boats will float even when swamped, and that it is far safer to stay with a swamped boat than to attempt to swim to shore. In the case of sailboats, it is often possible to right the boat and then sit on the floor of the cockpit. To right a boat, the first step is to get the sails down. The centerboard is then forced down all the way, thus providing a point of leverage for righting the hull. As the drawing shows, the crew should stand on the centerboard and apply downward pressure while holding on at the coaming. With the boat righted, the entire crew can usually sit inside the cockpit without sinking the boat.

In the unlikely event that a swamped sailboat isn't rescued right away, it may even be possible to bail it out. Stuff clothing, sail bags, or even sail into the top of the centerboard well, and hang onto the

---

WHAT TO DO WHEN BOAT HAS CAPSIZED

Swim back to boat at once.

STAY WITH THE BOAT.

Put on life jackets, take off footwear and excess clothing.

Lash all loose gear together.

Remove sails.

Right boat if possible.

outside of the boat. If the waves are not too high, you may be able to splash and bail water from the cockpit fast enough to stay ahead of incoming water. Bailing out a swamped boat is time-consuming and exhausting work, however, and should only be tried as a last resort. It is much better to save your strength and wait for rescue.

12. Returning to Port

Having completed our imaginary cruise, it is time to return to port. This means sailing the boat up to and picking up a mooring, or sailing the boat up to a dock or into a slip. These may seem like very simple tasks. In reality, however, they may be difficult maneuvers. In any event, they require a thorough knowledge of the wind, the tide or current, and the sailing characteristics of the boat. To put it candidly, the skipper had better "know his stuff" or he is in for trouble.

A word of advice is in order at this point. Sooner or later you will acquire enough skill to master the art of sailing a boat up to a dock or into a slip. Until you do, however, be extremely cautious about approaching a dock or slip under sail. If your boat is small enough to be managed easily with oars or paddles, do not be ashamed to drop the sails and paddle up to the dock. Many a beginner has seriously damaged his boat by ramming it into a dock because he failed to correctly judge the wind or the momentum (the "carry") of the boat. The need for caution is especially great in the close quarters of many marinas. Time after time I have watched inexperienced sailors ram their sailboats into pilings, floating docks, or other boats in crowded marinas. If you are the least bit doubtful about your ability and the amount of room available, you will earn the respect of all the boatmen in the marina by paddling your boat in (or bringing it in under power).

Let me offer one other piece of advice at this point. Often, approaching or leaving a marina means sailing through a narrow channel. This is fine if you can sail downwind, but you may be a source of great annoyance to other boatmen if you have to tack upwind through the channel. The rules of the road give the sailboat under sail alone the right of way over power boats of a similar size, but demanding this right in a narrow channel can be a great imposition. If the traffic is heavy, and you must go upwind through a channel, find some way other than sailing to do it.

Now let's look at the techniques involved in getting a boat back to its berth and securing all gear until the next sail.

The technique of picking up the mooring. Whenever possible, the jib should be lowered and bagged before the final approach to the mooring.

As you will learn, careful attention to routine maintenance procedures at the end of each sail is a necessary evil. Without it, you spoil much of the fun of sailing, and run the risk of both accidents and expensive repairs.

APPROACHING A MOORING

A great many boats are stored on moorings between sails. A mooring is simply a large, permanently placed anchor from which chain and line lead to a floating buoy. Depending upon the area available, there may be plenty of room or very little room for maneuvering between boats tied up to moorings. As a small-boat skipper, you will no doubt use just your own mooring. Thus, once you get accustomed to it, you should have no trouble. Cruising boat skippers, on the other hand, often "borrow" moorings in strange ports, and must be able to adapt to varying conditions.

The basic tactic in approaching and picking up a mooring is quite simple. The idea is to approach the mooring float with the bow into the wind, judging the "shoot into the wind" so that the boat comes to a

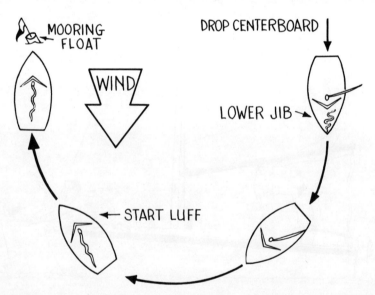

Approaching the mooring. The procedure is to round up into the wind and come to a dead halt just as the bow of the boat reaches the mooring.

dead stop just as it reaches the float. In the ideal case, a crew member up forward will pick up the mooring float just as the boat stops dead in the water. This takes practice and requires a knowledge of how the boat reacts in winds of varying strength. In general, small centerboard boats require one to two boat lengths in light winds to come up into the wind, while about three boat lengths should be allowed in heavier winds. Keel boats, being heavier, have greater momentum than centerboard boats, and require about half again as much distance to come to a stop.

The drawing shows the general tactic in approaching the mooring. Whether running, reaching, or beating, the boat is turned up into the wind so that it glides forward to the mooring with sails luffing. If you are running, it will be necessary to swing to a reach before shooting up into the wind. As simple as this sounds, however, it isn't the entire story. Several other steps must also be taken to guarantee a smooth and successful approach. First, the centerboard should be dropped all the way before the approach to the mooring. This aids in steering and increases the stability of the boat. Second, drop and remove the jib if your boat handles well under mainsail alone. This gives the crew forward more room to work, and permits you to take the mooring float from either the port or the starboard side. Do not remove the jib if the boat handles sluggishly under main alone, or if you are coming in under very light winds.

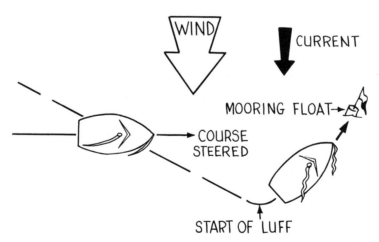

Approaching the mooring with wind and current from the same direction. In this instance a tight turn is necessary, for the boat will not carry very far against both the current and the wind.

Two potentially difficult situations at the mooring call for special mention. They are as follows: wind and strong tidal current coming from the same direction; wind and tide opposing each other with tidal current stronger. In the first instance, because the effect of the wind and tide add together, it is necessary to steer very close to the mooring before shooting into the wind. If the turn is too wide, the boat will fail to carry far enough. In addition, this is one of the times when the jib should be left up. The extra drive it imparts to the boat is required to counter the adverse tide.

In the second case, that is, when the wind and tide are opposed, but the tidal current is the stronger of the two, the safest way to approach the mooring is to drift down on it. The skipper should plan to luff up at least four boat lengths away from the mooring. Once stopped, head to wind, the boat will slowly drift toward the mooring under the influence of the tide. Completing this maneuver successfully calls for good timing. The skipper or crew must be ready to drop the sails the moment the mooring float has been taken aboard, for at this point the boat will swing around stern to the wind. If the sails are still up, they will fill immediately and be difficult to get down. Moreover, the boat is apt to sail about on the mooring and may jibe.

APPROACHING A DOCK

Although most sailboats are kept on a mooring, some are tied up to docks for the sake of convenience. Many modern marinas are equipped with floating docks that ride up and down with the tide. It is relatively easy to secure a boat to these. Permanent docks and pilings are also still in use, however. Tying a boat up to these requires special attention. The skipper should be familiar with the range of the tide in the area and should adjust his docking lines to allow for tidal changes. I remember a skipper who very carefully snugged his boat up tight at low tide, confident that he had done the right thing. Eight hours later he was astonished at the beating the boat had taken after the tide had come in on the heels of a strong breeze. As you will see later, if a boat is tied up correctly this type of damage needn't happen.

It's also important to use fenders or bumpers when tying up to a dock. The constant chafing of hull against dock can be very damaging to a paint job or the gel coat of a fiberglass hull.

Even if you do not keep your boat at a dock, the time will come when you will have to approach and land at a dock under sail. Again, a bit of advice. If you are in doubt, and conditions will allow it, drop the sails and paddle up to the dock. If you must sail in, however, keep one basic rule in mind. Always approach a dock with the bow of the boat into the wind, unless there is a strong current going against the wind. As the drawing shows, coming to a stop at a dock after shooting up into the wind is just as precise a maneuver as picking up a mooring.

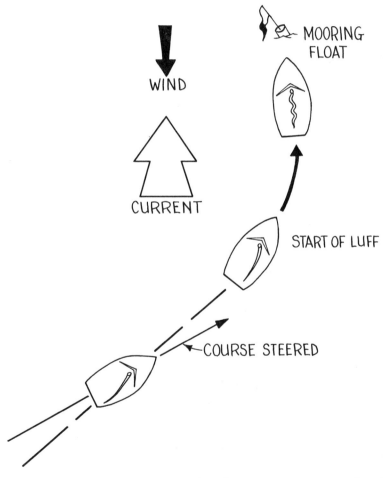

Approaching the mooring with wind and current opposite each other, but with the current stronger. The boat is luffed up and brought to a stop upwind of the mooring. It then drifts down on the mooring.

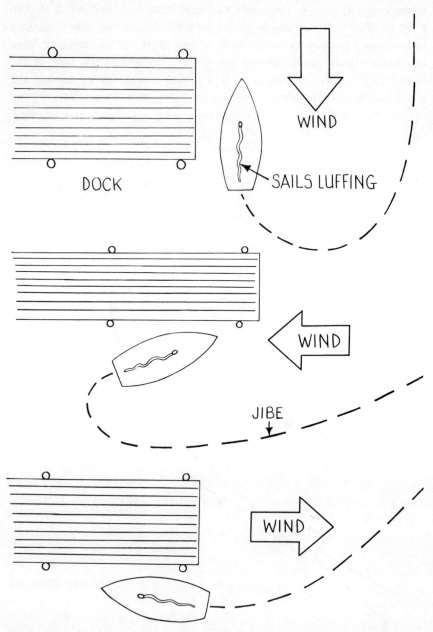

Approaching a dock under sail. If possible, always head into the wind and bring the boat to a stop just as it reaches the dock.

The one difference is that if the skipper misjudges his speed, he runs the risk of ramming the dock or another boat.

If a strong current is running against the wind, the dock should be approached on a run from the windward direction under jib alone. Then, just before landing, the jib is dropped to kill headway. This also is a tactic that requires caution. Once the sails are down completely, the boat will become difficult to handle. If the landing is not successful, the boat could drift into other boats before control is restored by raising sail.

In the unlikely event that you must approach a dock from its windward side (a lee dock), the safest maneuver is to luff up some distance from the dock, drop anchor, and lower the sails. As the drawing shows, you then pay out anchor line, which permits the boat to drift back toward the dock. The anchor should be left in place, of course, for it can be used to haul the boat away from the dock when it is time to leave.

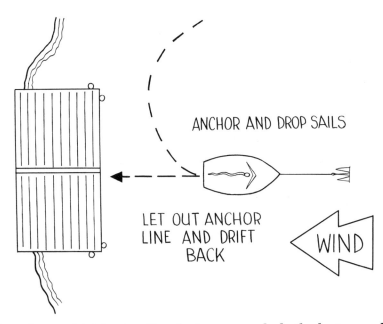

ANCHOR AND DROP SAILS

LET OUT ANCHOR LINE AND DRIFT BACK

WIND

When the wind is blowing directly down on a dock, the best procedure is to luff up off the dock, drop anchor, and then back down to the dock by paying out anchor line.

TYING UP CORRECTLY

For a quick and easy lesson in how *not* to tie up to a dock or in a slip, just visit any busy marina. Many of the boatmen (including sailors) who pull in for supplies, ice, fuel, or what have you, will demonstrate an impressive variety of incorrect ways to tie up. A bowline and possibly a stern line will usually do for a short stay at the dock. (Now is a good time to review knots, bends, and hitches. Can you tie all of them?)

For a longer stay, the safety of the boat under a variety of conditions must be considered. For example, a wind shift may cause the boat to bang against the dock. The wakes of passing boats can also pose a problem; often a wake can set a docked boat swinging back and forth. If it is not tied up properly, damage to the hull may be the result.

The drawing shows the proper lines to use when mooring broadside. The *bow* and *stern* lines are made fast to the nearest cleat forward and aft. They hold the boat in position broadside to the dock. Bow and stern lines should never be set up tight in tidal waters. Enough slack must be allowed for the rise and fall of the tide.

The spring lines serve another purpose. They prevent the boat from surging back and forth at the dock. To be most effective, they should be as nearly parallel to the dock as possible. As the drawing shows, the *after spring line* runs from the foredeck cleat all the way to the dock cleat *aft* of the boat. The *forward spring line* then runs from a stern cleat to the dock cleat *forward* of the boat. Shorter spring lines may be used, but they become less effective as the angle between the line and the dock increases. You will often be tempted to skip the spring lines and make do with just the bow and stern lines. For a short stay in relatively quiet waters, this may be adequate. On the other hand, if there is any traffic in the channel near your boat and you intend to stay awhile, it is much wiser to rig the spring lines. For an overnight stay, the spring lines are a must. And don't forget fenders. Without them, you run the risk of badly scarring the finish on the hull.

Tying up in a slip, that is, stern to a dock with the bow between two pilings, poses an altogether different problem. In this case, the trick is to arrange the docking lines so that the boat is held off the dock, and also securely between the pilings. In addition, the stern must be held in place, so that it does not sway back and forth or into the adjacent slip.

The drawing shows how to rig the lines. First, note the arrangement of the stern lines. These are led from the stern cleats on the boat out

TYING UP BROADSIDE

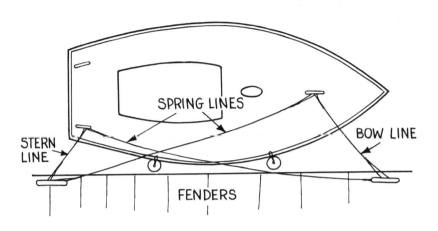

TYING UP   IN A SLIP

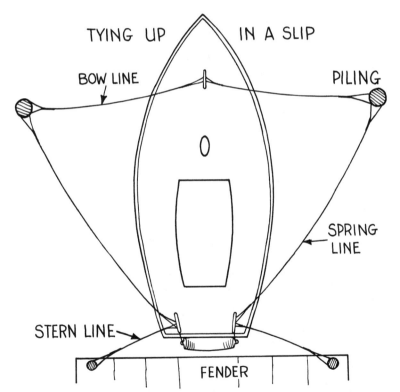

How to tie up broadside to a dock and in a slip. The lines must all be placed carefully to prevent damage to the boat.

parallel to the dock; if set properly, this prevents the stern from swaying from side to side. The spring lines are rigged from the stern cleats to the pilings. They hold the stern of the boat away from the dock. Finally, the bow lines keep the bow of the boat centered between the pilings. The bow lines should be at about right angles to the center line of the boat to effectively hold the boat in position. If your boat is too long to do this from the bow cleat, rig the lines from the base of the mast instead. It is sometimes quite difficult to tie up in a slip. Often the pilings are so far apart that reaching them becomes a problem. In addition, water turbulence may bob the boat about so that keeping your balance while tying up is difficult.

SECURING THE BOAT

Our sail is over. Skipper and crew are refreshed, but pleasantly fatigued, and ready to call it a day. The natural instinct at this point is to pick up personal gear and go home; the final tidying up that the boat obviously needs can be taken care of before the next sail. Don't give in to this urge. If you let these "housekeeping" chores go, you face a dirty, cluttered, and generally unshipshape boat when you are ready to go out the next time. The mess never seems like much when you leave it. When you come back, however, it seems much worse because it stands in the way of the pleasure you want right away—*not* after forty-five minutes or more of cleaning up.

Let's run through the various chores you should complete before leaving the boat. First, the sails should be bagged. Be sure to remove all battens before stowing the sails in their bags. Coil and secure the jibsheets. Drop the boom into the boom crutch, and tighten the mainsheet to hold it securely in place. Coil the mainsheet. Check both the jib and main halyards—be sure they are securely cleated down. If your boat is moored in a location where other boatmen sleep overnight, run an elastic shock cord around each halyard and the shroud closest to it. This will hold the halyards away from the mast and prevent them from slapping. The sound of halyards slapping against masts is most disconcerting to those who are trying to sleep.

If your boat has a removable rudder and tiller assembly, remove it and stow it away. If the rudder is rigged to stay in place between sails, lash the tiller to prevent the rudder from banging back and forth. Pump and sponge out the bilge. Make fast all loose gear, such as paddles,

THE FRIENDSHIP SLOOP

The Friendship Sloop is one of the best known small working sailboats of the United States. These lovely boats are termed "Friendships"
because so many of them were built at the little harbor of Friendship,
Maine, on Muscongus Bay. Originally fishing boats, Friendship sloops
today enjoy a renewed popularity as pleasure yachts. In fact, an as-
sociation, The Friendship Sloop Society, has been formed to bring together owners of these interesting sailboats. Friendship sloops are deep-
keeled boats with the ballast carried inside and very low. Thus the boats
were designed to sail with very little angle of heel, even when sailing
to windward in a blow. They are exceptionally seaworthy, as the clipper
bow, strong sheer, and counter stern shown on the boat above suggest.
(Photo by Peter Barlow)

life jackets, bilge pump, and battens. Haul the centerboard all the way up. If the centerboard is left down, it will bang back and forth in the centerboard trunk as the boat moves about at the mooring.

Collect all trash and the leftovers from your picnic lunch. Do not throw any of this in the water. Virtually all marinas and yacht clubs supply large trash bins. Use them. There is nothing worse than a mooring area or marina fouled by floating garbage and trash. Clean up topsides and deck. Don't forget to take the "cooler" with you, especially if it contained fruit juice or iced tea. If it held fresh water, and there is some left over, salt-water sailors should use it to sponge down the topside varnished woodwork. This removes the salt residue and prolongs the life of the varnish.

Finally, make a last check to be sure the mooring line is securely fastened and that it runs through a bow chock. Also make sure the mooring float is tightly lashed down on the foredeck. The last task before leaving the boat is fastening the cockpit cover in place.

That does it. The boat is now in shipshape condition. You can go home confident that you have done everything possible to prevent damage while the boat is at the mooring. You also know that everything is ready to go the next time you are ready to sail.

13. Anchors and Anchoring

Instead of sending you into port during the previous chapter, we might have lengthened our imaginary cruise by getting into anchors and anchoring. This we decided not to do, for the problems of anchoring require a separate chapter.

Anchoring is an important part of boating. All boats should have at least one anchor aboard, together with enough line for the waters the boat customarily operates on. While one anchor is usually enough for smaller boats, at least two should be kept aboard larger boats. In the absence of a better rule, for temporary daytime anchoring, plan to use about one-half pound of anchor for each foot of boat length. For example, a nine- or ten-pound Danforth anchor would be quite adequate for an eighteen-to-twenty-foot boat during a picnic lunch under relatively good conditions. On the other hand, a larger boat anchoring overnight should use a heavier anchor to guard against dragging while the crew is asleep. Sailors often refer to their lighter anchor as the "lunch hook." Not many are willing to sleep over on a lunch hook; there is too great a possibility of dragging.

As you have probably gathered by now, there is more to anchoring than just tossing a weight on a line overboard. Many factors must be taken into account when anchoring. What does the bottom consist of? Is it rocky, sandy, or covered with seaweed or mud? Is the anchor to be used correct for the type of bottom? How deep is the water? Will the boat stay afloat at dead low tide? Is there enough anchor line to give adequate *scope* (the length of anchor line needed for the anchor to hold), particularly when the tide comes in? How will the boat swing around in relation to other anchored boats should the wind or tide change? Is the spot chosen for anchoring protected from wind and sea? If you satisfy yourself on all of these counts, the chances are that you will be safely and securely anchored.

TYPES OF GROUND TACKLE

Many different types of anchors are available. We have chosen to describe four of the more popular types. These are anchors you are likely to see in use on small boats. They have different characteristics, all of which must be considered when an anchor is chosen.

The *yachtsman's* anchor, although awkward to handle and store, offers the best holding power in different types of bottom. It is particularly good in a rocky bottom. This anchor is somewhat heavier than other more modern anchors for the same holding power. The drawing shows the yachtsman's anchor opened for use and folded down for storage. The *Danforth* anchor has exceptionally good power, although it is quite light in weight. For this reason, it has become very popular. As you shop around for an anchor, you will discover many that are simple variations of the Danforth idea. For a general-purpose anchor for sandy or muddy bottom, the Danforth is your best choice.

Two types of *mushroom* anchors are shown. The anchor on many permanent moorings is a very large and heavy mushroom. As the drawing shows, two types are often seen on small boats. One has a long, thin shank, the other a short, stubby shank. Mushrooms are easy to use because there are no flukes for the anchor line to tangle on. In addition, they hold well in muddy bottoms. Many skippers of small racing sailboats carry a mushroom anchor. This anchor is used in a race to prevent drifting when the wind drops and the tide is running the wrong way. The *navy* type anchor is shown here because it is often offered for sale to small-boat owners. It should not, however, be used on small boats. This type of anchor depends more on weight than on digging in for holding power. As a result, it is more useful on larger vessels. In the smaller sizes, the short flukes do not dig deeply enough to hold well. Thus the anchor simply drags through the surface layers of mud or sand.

COMMON ANCHORS

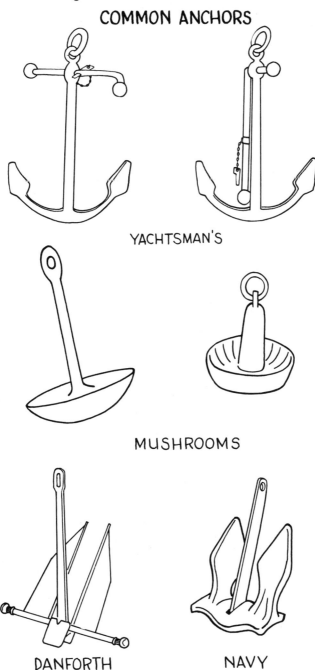

YACHTSMAN'S

MUSHROOMS

DANFORTH   NAVY

Several different types of common anchors. For sandy or muddy bottoms, the Danforth holds best and is the lightest.

CHOOSING AN ANCHORAGE

Unless you know a location thoroughly, deciding where to "drop the hook" can be a problem. Despite the unknown factors of a strange anchorage, however, there are certain guidelines that will help you whenever you wish to anchor. First, very carefully survey the harbor or bay you have selected. This means sailing around the anchorage until you know its characteristics, and until you find the quiet and sheltered side. You should select a spot that is protected from the prevailing winds as well as from the larger waves that sweep into the harbor from open water. Check the weather report for wind velocity and direction. This, of course, will have a bearing on where you anchor. For example, if the prevailing winds are southwest, you would ordinarily look for a spot to the northeast of a group of small islands. But suppose an easterly wind or storm is predicted. Under these circumstances an anchorage northeast of the island would be exposed. Your stay would be uncomfortable at least, and possibly dangerous should the wind really kick up.

If you are sailing a small boat, look for a spot close to shore. With the centerboard up, you will be able to move in very close indeed. Since keel boats cannot anchor too close to shore, you should find plenty of room. If it becomes necessary to anchor among other boats, choose a spot among boats the same size as your own. Try to anchor at least three to four boat lengths away from the nearest boat. This will allow enough room for swinging on the wind or tide.

Whenever possible, you should also study a chart of the anchorage area before selecting a spot. The chart will indicate the depth of the water at low tide and the nature of the bottom. As you well realize, both of these factors are important. It is rather senseless, for example, to expect a Danforth anchor to hold on a rocky bottom when the obvious choice is the yachtsman's anchor.

DROPPING THE ANCHOR

For some obscure reason most boating beginners think the way to put an anchor down is to throw it as far away from the boat as possible. This is incorrect. Whenever an anchor is thrown, there is a possibility the line will foul on the flukes; as a result, the anchor will not take hold. A good seaman (1) makes sure the anchor line is fastened to the boat, (2) frees the line on deck to avoid entanglement, and (3) *lowers* the anchor over the side when the skipper gives the command.

The sequence of steps is quite simple, and is easy to master. The skipper puts his crew forward to handle anchor and line just as soon as he has chosen a spot. He then brings the boat up into the wind so that it stops dead in the water directly over the spot selected. At his command, the crew then lowers the anchor to the bottom and pays out line as the boat begins to drift backward. After he has payed out enough line to equal three or four times the depth of the water, he holds the line momentarily to make the anchor dig in. Enough additional line is then payed out to get the correct *scope,*

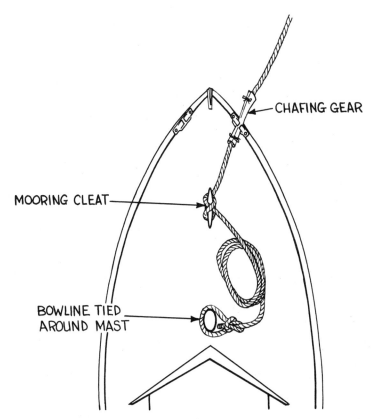

CHAFING GEAR

MOORING CLEAT

BOWLINE TIED
AROUND MAST

How to doubly secure the anchor line. If the boat is to remain at anchor for any length of time, chafing gear at the bow chock is advisable.

and the line is cleated down. If you intend to leave the boat anchored for any period of time, make the anchor line doubly fast by fastening its end around the mast behind the cleat on the foredeck.

SCOPE

If you will look back at the drawings of anchors, you will see that it is necessary for the shank of most anchors to be parallel to the bottom for the flukes to take hold. But the shank can only remain parallel to the bottom if the pull of the anchor line is sideways. A sideways pull can be accomplished one way only. This is by paying out enough anchor line so that it lies parallel to the bottom where it ties into the anchor. It generally takes a length of line from four to seven times the depth of the water to insure that the anchor will hold. This length of line is called the *scope*. If there is any doubt about whether an anchor will hold, the wisest move is to increase scope. Of course, if other anchored boats are too close, there is a limit to the amount of scope you can use.

As you can see, the trick is to prevent any upward pull on the shank of the anchor. Increasing scope will do it. But there is another way also. This is to add weight to the anchor line so that it holds the anchor's shank down. The drawing shows a popular way to do

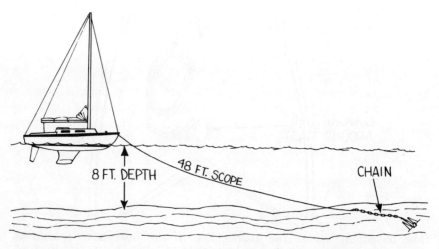

8 FT. DEPTH   48 FT. SCOPE   CHAIN

Scope is the length of anchor line compared to the depth of the water. For most types of bottom, a scope of six to one will be adequate.

the job. Simply add a short length of galvanized chain between the anchor and anchor line. About four to six feet of quarter-inch chain should work quite well for an eighteen-to-twenty-foot boat. Marine supply stores, in fact, sell such lengths of chain coated with rubber. The rubber protects the iron from rusting and also keeps the chain from scarring the finish of the boat.

Keep in mind that you drop the anchor some four to six times the depth of the water forward of the spot you have chosen for the boat. That is, the boat will ride below the point where the anchor is actually dropped overboard. If your judgment is good, the boat will come to rest close to the three to four boat lengths from the nearest boat that you planned on. If your judgment is poor, you will have to try again. Every anchorage has its inept skipper—the fellow who never succeeds in anchoring his boat free of other boats.

Let's assume you have the anchor down and that you think there is enough scope for it to hold. How do you make sure? The answer is simple; take *bearings* on shore to see if the boat moves. The drawing shows how this is done. Look directly abeam of the boat, and line up two objects on shore. Remember the two objects, and then check their position in fifteen minutes or so. If they remain in line, the anchor is not dragging. Check every hour or so, and if the boat swings on the tide or wind, take new bearings after it has come to its new position.

WEIGHING ANCHOR

Leaving an anchorage is similar to leaving a mooring, with one or two minor differences. The first thing to do is to prepare the mainsail for raising. Next, the crew should go forward to haul in the anchor line until it is very nearly vertical. At this point the main should be raised (it is assumed that the boat is pointing into the wind while riding at anchor). The sail will luff, of course. Next haul up the anchor, but do not take it on deck immediately. You can dunk the anchor in the water to wash the mud away, or even swab it away. Take the anchor on deck only after it has been thoroughly cleaned.

At this point the skipper can allow the bow to fall off, and then sail away on a reach if there is sufficient room. If there is too little room, the jib should be raised immediately after the anchor has been lifted clear of the water. With the jib up, it can be put aback to determine the course the boat will take. Under both jib and main, the skipper has better control of the boat as he sails free of other anchored boats. The final step is to coil the anchor line and stow it below decks along with the anchor.

Sometimes, if you have been anchored in a very muddy bottom, the anchor sticks tight. Despite hauling on the anchor line by skipper and crew, it won't come out. This is indeed a problem, and if your boat does not have an engine, it can really interfere with your sailing plans. There is a simple trick, however, that usually succeeds when hauling fails. Have everybody on board the boat come forward to the bow. This, of course, makes the bow ride very low in the water. Now haul in the anchor line until it is taut and straight up and down. Cleat the line tightly, and then move the entire crew aft to

TAKING A BEARING ON SHORE TO MAKE SURE ANCHOR ISN'T DRAGGING

To check your position while at anchor, take a bearing on shore. Line up two objects abeam of the boat and check periodically to make sure the bearing has not changed.

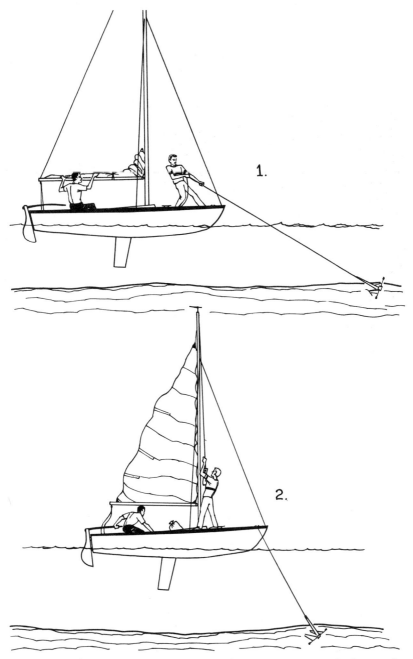

The steps in weighing anchor. First, shorten scope until the anchor line is nearly vertical. Then raise the main, haul up the anchor, and sail away.

the stern. Shifting the weight aft will drive the stern down and the bow up. Very frequently this is enough to lift the imbedded anchor clear of the mud.

Up to this point we have assumed that the boat is pointing into the wind on the anchor. This is usually the situation, for the wind is generally stronger than the current. Sometimes, however, the current is stronger than the wind. When this happens the boat points downwind on the anchor line, presenting a problem when it comes time to weigh anchor.

This is one of the very few times when a sail is raised downwind. Raise the jib and take in just enough sheet for the sail to fill and carry the boat forward toward the anchor. Haul the anchor line as the boat moves forward, and take the anchor aboard as quickly as

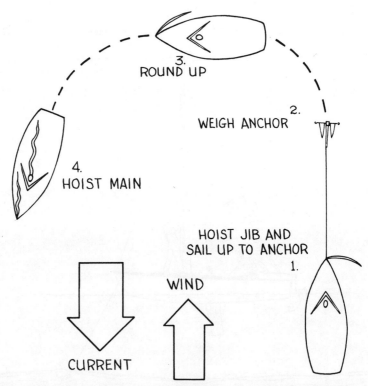

When a boat lies at anchor to the current, hoist the jib first and sail down to the anchor. After weighing anchor, the boat is headed up into the wind to hoist the mainsail.

possible. Keep running on jib alone until the boat is clear of all other boats. At this point round the boat up into the wind, raise the main quickly, put the jib aback, and sail off on the course you have selected.

14. Reading the Weather

There is an old saying that goes as follows: "The good seaman weathers the storm he cannot avoid, and he avoids the storm he cannot weather." We have already discussed sailing tactics in heavy weather, and now we want to emphasize the importance of learning how to "read" the weather. If there is one single factor that dominates sailing, it is the weather. Thus the knowledgeable sailor is always prepared on three counts: (1) he never goes out without obtaining the latest weather report, (2) while sailing, he continually watches for indications of an adverse weather change, and (3) when such a weather change seems probable, he takes appropriate action at once. He does not wait, thinking (usually incorrectly) that the change won't occur for a while, or that he has plenty of time before the storm or squall hits.

Keeping on top of the weather is by no means as difficult as it may seem. This is particularly true of obtaining weather reports before going out, for a number of sources are readily available. Virtually every newspaper contains a daily weather map that gives the weather situation throughout the entire country. What is just as important, however, is that these maps allow rough weather predictions for up to a day or so in advance. Become familiar with the map in your local paper. Learn the symbols, and study the map daily for a period of weeks or months. This will establish in your mind the normal weather patterns for your area, and enable you to make a reasonably good prediction on any given day. Television weather reports and forecasts are perhaps even better, for they provide a more up-to-date analysis of the local situation. Many of these programs, as you know, include a thorough weather-map analysis. If you plan to go sailing the following day, make it a practice to watch the TV weather report the night before.

Radio forecasts are also important. You are no doubt familiar with the brief forecasts given often during regular programing. What you may not know is that many stations in coastal areas broadcast periodic marine weather forecasts. These reports are quite thorough; they are essential to the careful sailor. If you cannot find station listings for marine forecasts in the paper, call your local Coast Guard station for the necessary information.

This photo of hurricane Gladys (October 1968) taken from the Apollo 7 spacecraft clearly shows the counterclockwise movement of the air around the "eye" of the storm. The photo was taken about 150 miles southwest of Tampa, Florida, at an altitude of ninety-seven nautical miles. (Photo by NASA)

A good barometer is also very useful. This instrument, as you probably know, measures the pressure exerted by the atmosphere. In general, the drier the air, the greater the pressure it exerts. Thus a rising barometer often means clearing, with fair weather ahead. A falling barometer, on the other hand, usually means bad weather, with rain and cloudy conditions. Do not rely on a barometer if you have access to other, more reliable sources of weather information. A barometer allows a very rough forecast only; it should not be looked upon as an infallible instrument.

As you will see later in this chapter, clouds are also good indicators of what the weather holds. There are many different types of clouds, although just three types are enough to provide visible evidence of what is taking place, and what is to take place shortly. Cloud changes, in particular, are useful for signaling weather changes while you are out on the water. In fact, if you have been out sailing for many hours, and you do not have a radio on board, the clouds are probably the only indication you have of an impending weather change. We will see just how shortly.

WEATHER PATTERNS

Weather systems in the United States move from west to east. This general movement is caused by the westerlies—prevailing winds that result from the earth's rotation. In addition, the heating effect of the sun and the interaction of high- and low-pressure areas produce weather changes.

As you may know, the weather we experience is the result of alternating high- and low-pressure areas passing overhead. That is, "lows" are usually followed by "highs." When the pressure is high, the weather is generally good. On the other hand, the weather is usually poor when a low is centered overhead.

Highs and lows are characterized by a particular type of air movement. As the drawing shows, the wind blows in a clockwise direction around a high, but also toward the outside. This is called *anticyclonic rotation*. The wind around a low, on the other hand, blows in a counterclockwise direction in toward the low-pressure center. This movement is called *cyclonic rotation*. A hurricane is simply a cyclonic storm of great intensity. As the warm, moist air rotates toward the center of any low system, the air begins to rise. But in rising it is cooled. Then, when sufficient cooling has occurred, moisture condenses and clouds and rain result.

A closer look at the diagram will suggest one or two additional clues to the weather. For example, along the East Coast strong northeast winds usually mean increasing cloudiness and rain. In New England such storm systems are referred to as "nor'easters." When the wind then shifts to northwest, it usually means the passage of a low and the approach of a high. Clearing generally follows, and fair weather can be expected until the next low arrives.

So far we have described the air mass movements that produce weather changes over very wide areas. The wind of a nor'easter and the brisk northwest breeze that follows passage of a cold front are results of these major air movements. On a smaller scale, the sailor can also look for two types of local breezes, both of which can affect

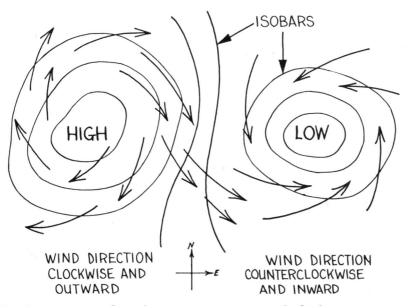

Weather patterns flow from west to east, with high-pressure areas alternating with low-pressure areas. This diagram shows how the winds blow around lows and highs. An isobar is a line drawn through points of equal barometric pressure.

his sailing pleasure. These two breezes are called the *land breeze* and the *sea breeze*.

Land and sea breezes occur near the coastline. Indeed, the story is that fore-and-aft rigs were originally developed in this country to

When boats are sailing very close together, as in this race, it is absolutely essential that the rules of the road be understood and applied. Knowledge of the rules of the road becomes more important each year as increasing numbers of boats appear on our waterways. (Photo by Dorothy I. Crossley)

take advantage of the land and sea breezes along our seacoasts and on the Great Lakes. These breezes develop because water and land differ in their capacity to absorb and hold heat. Water absorbs heat from the sun much more slowly than land, but it also holds the heat much longer. Let's start our description at a point in time when the water and land temperatures are about the same—an hour or so before midnight.

As the night hours pass, the land continues to cool. The water just offshore, however, does not lose heat as fast. The result is that around midnight the air above the water is warmer than the air above the adjacent land area. But warm air rises. Thus the air above the water rises, and the cooler air over the land area moves in beneath it. This cool air in motion off the land is the land breeze. Of course, as the cool air comes in contact with the warmer water, it is also warmed. It then rises, and the cycle continues.

After sunrise, the land warms up rapidly. On a bright, sunny day it is usually warmer than the adjacent water sometime around noon. At this point a sea breeze begins. The warm air over the land rises, and cooler air moves off the water to take its place. Anyone who has been to the beach on a bright, warm day is familiar with sea

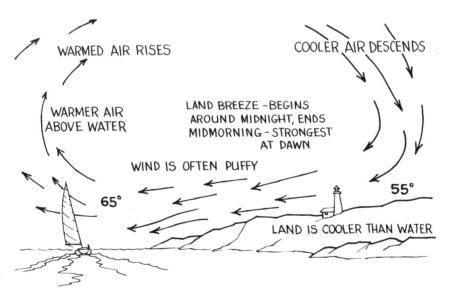

How a land breeze is generated. The warmer air above the water rises, and the cooler air above the land moves under it.

breezes. They usually blow briskly through the afternoon, and then die down around sundown. The greater the temperature difference between land and water, the stronger the breeze.

Many sailors have learned to depend upon afternoon sea breezes to get them home. On Long Island Sound, for example, the afternoon sea breeze from the south is practically a tradition. Local sailors call it the "homing" breeze; they are greatly disappointed if it does not appear "on time" to get them into port before dusk.

FRONTS

With major air masses rotating around highs and lows, contact between two masses of air with differing temperatures is inevitable. Such a collision is called a *front*. There are four types of front—*cold, warm, occluded,* and *stationary.*

As far as the sailor is concerned, the cold front is the most important, for it is usually accompanied by violent thunderstorms. A cold front is produced when a cold air mass meets and thrusts under

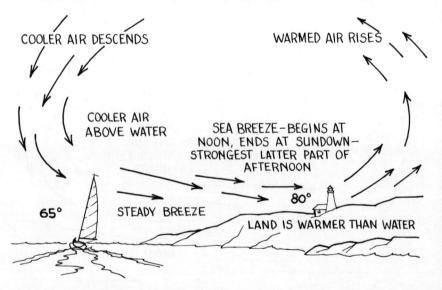

How a sea breeze is generated. The warmer air over the land rises, then the cooler air over the water moves in under it. Late afternoon sea breezes are often a great help in getting back to home port.

a warm air mass. Because the colder air is heavier, it stays close to the ground, but forces the warm, moist air rapidly to high altitudes. As the warm air rises and cools, its moisture condenses, forming thunderhead clouds. Severe thunderstorms often result.

A warm front results when warm air rides up and over a mass of cold air. The warm air, usually laden with moisture, then cools, and the moisture condenses. Cloudiness and rain are the result. Sometimes a fast-moving cold front will overtake a warm front moving in the same direction. When this happens, the cold air in front and behind the warm air forces the warm air upward. This is called an occluded front. Such fronts may behave as cold fronts or warm fronts or both. Finally, when a cold front and a warm front meet head on and interlock, the result is a stationary front. It helps to know the type of weather frontal conditions will bring. In particular, you should be wary of any approaching cold front, for the thunderstorms it brings are often very severe and dangerous.

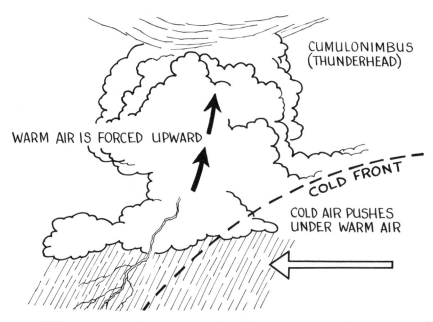

A cold front exists when a mass of cold air pushes under a mass of warmer air. As the warmer air rises, violent thunderstorms often develop.

Of the many different cloud types, three are of particular importance to the sailor. These are the *cumulonimbus,* or thunderhead; the *cumulus;* and the *cirrus* clouds. Cumulonimbus clouds are the massive vertical thunderhead clouds associated with the violent thunderstorms mentioned earlier. All sailors must learn to recognize these clouds, for the storms they bring can be very dangerous to a boat under sail.

The typical thunderstorm occurs during the summer months, usually late in the day. These storms make their first appearance as a darkening sky, usually in the northwest. Often, however, the first warning of an approaching thunderstorm may be AM radio static. Static may develop up to ten hours prior to the storm itself. Following the darkening sky, the typical anvil-shaped, towering thunderhead appears. The cloud is dark and "dirty" along its bottom, with violent wind gusts, heavy rain, and whitecaps underneath. The top is anvil-shaped, but sometimes the cloud is so tall this formation isn't visible. Very often these storms advance in a sharply defined front—an awesome sight to anyone who has witnessed it at sea.

When the storm hits, usually no more than a half hour after one sights the thunderhead, there will be violent winds from several different directions and usually drenching rain. In one thunderstorm we rode out at anchor, the rain was so heavy it was impossible to see the stern of the boat from the cabin—a distance of some seven feet! Waves are generally not a problem, for these storms come up too quickly to generate much wave action.

The winds in thunderstorms are so violent and erratic it is very important to prepare properly for the arrival of the storm. *Under no circumstances should you attempt to sail through a thunderstorm.* If you are close enough to shore—be it a sandy beach, a sheltered cove, or home port—get in as quickly as possible, and get the sails down. If there isn't time to reach shore or home port, drop the sails and lash them down securely. Then anchor and stay put until the storm has passed over.

If the thunderstorms you are caught in are the result of isolated masses of hot air rising into colder air, you can expect them to pass over quickly. These are the typical late afternoon storms of a hot summer day. Storms associated with a cold front, however, may take longer to clear out. As you may know, these storms are spread out along the entire cold front. They are more violent than the local

CIRRUS "CHANGING WEATHER"

CUMULUS "FAIR WEATHER"

CUMULONIMBUS "THUNDERHEAD"

The cloud shapes and patterns you should learn to recognize. It is especially important that you learn to spot thunderheads before the thunderstorm arrives.

thunderstorm, but they can be avoided, for an advancing cold front is usually forecast well in advance.

Cumulus clouds are fair weather clouds. These are the bright, "cottony" clouds seen on fair, sunny days. They have softly rounded edges, but near the horizon they are flat along the bottom. As long as cumulus clouds are in the sky, there is little chance of any change in the weather. It pays to keep an eye on cumulus clouds, however. Sometimes one can grow tall enough to reach elevations where the temperature is below freezing. When this happens, the innocent fair weather cumulus cloud can develop into the dangerous cumulonimbus thunderhead cloud.

Cirrus clouds generally indicate a change in weather, usually for the worse. These clouds are thin and wispy. A sky with cirrus clouds is often called a "mare's tail" sky, because of its similarity to the feathery wisps of a streaming horse's tail. Cirrus clouds occur at altitudes of twenty thousand to twenty-five thousand feet. They often indicate cloudy, rainy weather within a day or so.

STORM WARNINGS

Always check the weather report before going out sailing. In addition, check for storm warnings at a nearby yacht club or marina. Administered by the U. S. Weather Bureau, storm warning stations are located along the East and West Coasts, on the Great Lakes, and in Hawaii and Puerto Rico. The warnings consist of flags or pennants for the daytime and lights for nighttime. As the illustration shows, there are four warnings—*small craft, gale, storm,* and *hurricane.* You should commit these signals to memory, and never forget to check before going out sailing.

The most important warning for the small-boat sailor is the small craft warning. This signal, when posted, covers a wide range of wind and/or sea conditions. In addition, the term "small craft" includes boats of many different sizes and types. To be on the safe side, always get a detailed weather forecast before going out when the small craft warning pennant is flying. Wind and sea conditions may or may not be too severe for your boat—you won't be able to tell from the warning signal alone. You will have to match experience with a detailed weather report to estimate the danger correctly. For example, on a given day wind and sea conditions might be very hazardous for a twenty-foot

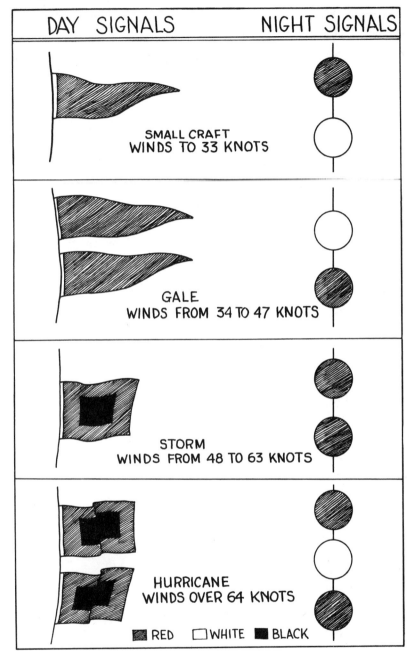

The official Weather Bureau Coastal Warning Display System. The night signals are lights. Be sure to get a complete weather forecast whenever small craft warnings are displayed; it may be too rough for your boat.

centerboard boat, but merely exciting and stimulating for a twenty-foot keel boat.

TIDE AND CURRENT

A brief word about the tides and the water movements they cause is in order at this point. Strictly speaking, *tide* is the vertical rise and fall of a body of water. Tide is caused by the gravitational pull of the moon, and to a lesser extent that of the sun, on a body of water. When the sun and the moon are in line with the earth, their combined pull is greater. Hence, the tidal range is greater. Such tides are called *spring tides*. On the other hand, when the sun, moon, and earth form a right angle in space—that is, when they are not in a line—the tidal range is smallest. These tides are called *neap tides*.

Current is the horizontal flow of water. When the tide changes at high tide, and the water begins to drop, it can only drop by flowing horizontally out of or away from the bay or inlet it had flooded. Current caused by tidal changes is called *tidal current*. The current of a river or stream is not associated in any way with the tide; it is caused by gravitational force only. Of course, many rivers that empty into the ocean experience tides. On the Connecticut River, for example, the effect of the tide is quite noticeable as far north as Hartford, a distance of some forty miles from the mouth of the river.

15. Rules of the Road and Aids to Navigation

One of the first things you will notice when you begin sailing is the traffic. America's recreational waterways are becoming more and more crowded every year. Unfortunately, along with the crowding there has been a noticeable increase in the number of accidents. Thus to enjoy sailing and to avoid accidents it becomes necessary to thoroughly master the traffic rules that govern the movements of boats. These rules are called the rules of the road; their fundamental purpose is to avoid collisions. The rules apply to all types of boats, and cover all of the possible types of meetings that can take place between two boats. In all of these instances the rules determine the boat that is *privileged* and the boat that is *burdened*. A privileged boat has the *right of way,* and is entitled to, and to a large extent is obligated to maintain course and speed. The burdened boat must look out for the privileged boat; it must alter course and/or speed so that it does not interfere with the privileged boat.

In almost all instances, a sailboat under sail alone has the right of way over a powerboat. This means that powerboats should stay clear of sailboats at all times. The important exceptions to this rule are as follows. A sailboat overtaking and passing a powerboat (or any boat, for that matter) is burdened; it must stay clear. Another exception refers to meetings between sailboats and very large powered vessels in restricted channels. Neither sailboats nor powerboats under sixty-five feet in length can claim the right of way over large, powered vessels that can navigate only inside a restricted channel. The safest

182

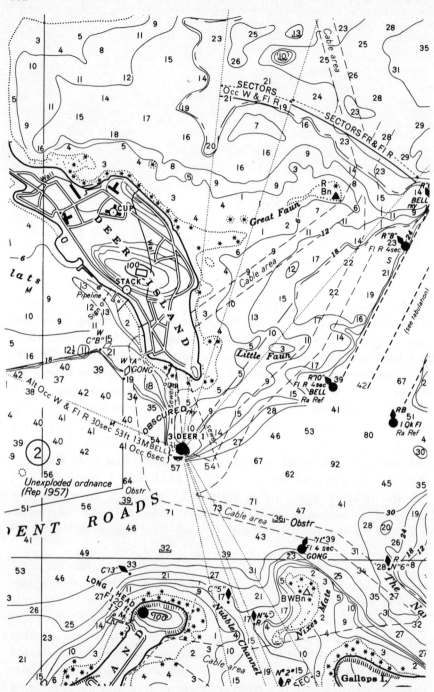

A small portion of a U. S. Coast and Geodetic Survey navigational chart.

application of this rule is to attempt to stay clear of all other vessels when sailing in a narrow channel. As we mentioned earlier, this situation will probably only occur if you attempt to tack upwind in a narrow channel. It is far better to find another way to get through the channel. Finally, remember that all other vessels, including sailboats under sail alone, must stay clear of fishing vessels using nets or lines or trawls.

An informal rule that you should take to heart and employ whenever you are in doubt is as follows: *Don't press your advantage!* With the very large number of inexperienced boatmen now crowding the waterways, you cannot count on the other man knowing the rules or correctly anticipating your intentions. We repeat: If you are in doubt about the situation, make every attempt to stay clear. Such common sense and courtesy will go a long way toward making your hours on the water both happy and safe.

RULES FOR BOATS UNDER SAIL ALONE

As you become familiar with the following rules, you will note that they favor the boat that is sailing closehauled. That is, the privileged boat is the one that is closehauled. This ruling dates back to the days of the square-riggers, vessels that sailed poorly to windward. Sailing closehauled was thus favored by the seafaring men who originally established the rules of the road.

The rules are as follows. Whenever two sailing vessels are approaching each other in such a way that there is a risk of collision, one of the vessels must stay clear. The possible situations and the rules are: (a) *A boat that is running free will stay clear of a boat that is closehauled.* The boat running free is burdened. (b) *A boat closehauled on the port tack will stay clear of a boat closehauled on the starboard tack.* The boat on the port tack is burdened. (c) *When both boats are running free, but with the wind on different sides, the boat that has the wind on the port side will stay clear of the other.* Again, the boat on the port tack is burdened. Remember it this way: port, red, danger, burdened. (d) *When both boats are running free, with the wind on the same side, the boat that is to windward will stay clear of the boat that is to leeward.* In this case, the boat that is upwind is burdened. (e) *A boat that has the wind aft will stay clear of the other vessel.*

It is very important that you learn these rules well and that you apply them. At the same time keep in mind that many boatmen will not know the rules and that you will be forced to assume the responsibility for preventing accidents. By all means be upset when you observe failure to abide by the rules of the road. And you will observe such failure. We can only say that education is the answer to this type of problem. You may find yourself in a position someday to help by participating in either the U. S. Power Squadron or Coast Guard Auxiliary safe-boating programs. We hope that you will respond when the opportunity presents itself. Also keep in mind that the rules given above *do not apply* to sailboats in a race. The racing rules differ somewhat from the rules above, and apply only to the boats in the race; they do not apply to boats that happen onto a racing course.

RULES FOR BOATS UNDER POWER

Many small sailboats use outboard engines as auxiliary power. Whenever your sailboat is being powered by an engine—even if the sails are up—the boat is a motorboat according to the law and must follow the motorboat rules of the road. These rules differ from the sailing rules. They are as follows: (a) *Two motorboats approaching each other head on should pass port side to port side.* When the skipper of one of the boats alters course to starboard to honor this rule, he should give one short blast on his horn. The other skipper should then acknowledge by returning the single short blast. In the event two boats are approaching each other and will pass starboard to starboard, two short blasts on the horn should be given to indicate that course is being altered to port. Wherever possible, the boats should pass port side to port side, although instances do occur when it is more practical to pass starboard side to starboard side. (b) *A motorboat having another boat in its danger zone (from dead ahead to two points abaft the starboard beam) must stay clear.* The drawing shows how the "danger zone" rule applies. It may even be necessary to stop or reverse direction to stay clear. (c) *Any boat leaving a slip, or a berth at a dock, has no rights until it is entirely clear.* This means that the boat leaving the slip or dock must consider itself burdened until it is completely clear of the dock and in open water.

Additional horn signals you should learn to recognize are (a) three

A VESSEL THAT IS RUNNING FREE SHALL KEEP OUT OF THE WAY OF A VESSEL THAT IS CLOSE HAULED	WIND AFT KEEP CLEAR **WIND** CLOSE HAULED PRIVILEGED
A VESSEL THAT IS CLOSE HAULED ON THE PORT TACK SHALL KEEP OUT OF THE WAY OF A VESSEL THAT IS CLOSE HAULED ON THE STARBOARD TACK	CLOSE HAULED PORT TACK KEEP CLEAR CLOSE HAULED STARBOARD TACK PRIVILEGED
WHEN BOTH ARE RUNNING FREE, WITH THE WIND ON DIFFERENT SIDES, THE VESSEL THAT HAS THE WIND ON THE PORT SIDE SHALL KEEP OUT OF THE WAY OF THE OTHER	RUNNING FREE WIND ON PORT SIDE - KEEP CLEAR WIND ON STARBOARD SIDE PRIVILEGED
WHEN BOTH ARE RUNNING FREE, WITH THE WIND ON THE SAME SIDE, THE VESSEL THAT IS TO THE WINDWARD SHALL KEEP OUT OF THE WAY OF THE VESSEL THAT IS TO THE LEEWARD	TO WINDWARD KEEP CLEAR RUNNING FREE WIND ON SAME SIDE - PRIVILEGED
A VESSEL THAT HAS THE WIND AFT SHALL KEEP OUT OF THE WAY OF THE OTHER VESSEL	RUNNING FREE KEEP CLEAR PRIVILEGED

The rules of the road when both vessels are under sail alone. Note that the rules favor the boat that is sailing closehauled.

short blasts—my boat is proceeding astern, and (b) four or more blasts—danger! (either an emergency or failure to understand another vessel's signal).

There isn't room, nor is there any need, to discuss in detail here the regulations covering the lights required on different types of vessels. As a small-boat sailor, you will probably sail at night only very rarely. If your boat is not equipped with running lights of any kind, there are just two things you should keep in mind. First, remember that the starboard running light is green, and that the port running light is red. With this in mind, you can usually identify the course another boat is sailing at night. Second, should it be necessary for you to sail at night, have a flashlight or lantern available. Then, at the approach of another boat, you should flash the light on your sails to indicate your position and approximate course and speed. If you intend to sail extensively at night, of course, full navigation lights will be required. In addition, you will have to learn the various light com-

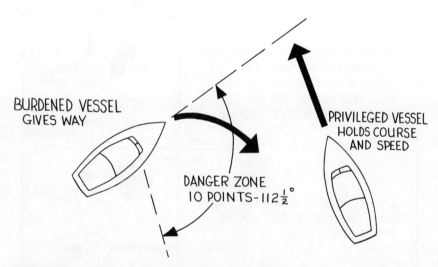

BURDENED VESSEL
GIVES WAY

PRIVILEGED VESSEL
HOLDS COURSE
AND SPEED

DANGER ZONE
10 POINTS-$112\frac{1}{2}°$

The "danger zone" rule for motorboats. Any boat that has another boat in its danger zone must give way. This means altering course, stopping, or even reversing if necessary.

THE NEW HAVEN SHARPIE

Experts believe that the New Haven Sharpie was introduced to the Connecticut oyster trade sometime around 1850, although flat-bottomed boats of this type had been in use in the United States since early colonial times. Sharpies were easy to construct. The sides were formed of two wide planks, and the bottom was cross-planked. These unusual working sailboats carried a distinctive rig, as shown here. Smaller ones carried a single mast. The sails were always tall and triangular, and resembled the modern jib-headed rig. Sharpies were very fast, and were often raced by the oyster fishermen. Note the correct position for flying the yacht ensign. (Photo by Peter Barlow)

binations used on other vessels. All of this information is contained in various Coast Guard pamphlets. These are free of charge from any Coast Guard office.

We shall briefly discuss three important *aids to navigation* in this chapter. These are *charts,* the *system of buoys* used on United States waters, and the *compass.* These three tools are indispensable to the sailor, especially the small-boat sailor who spends virtually all of his time on the waters near the shoreline. It is important to note that although charts, buoys, and the compass are called aids to navigation, their use in coastwise sailing is called *piloting.* To be more exact, piloting is close-to-shore navigation that uses visible landmarks, sound signals, and soundings. The visible landmarks the sailor uses include buoys, light signals, and distinctive structures on land. For example, once a sailor becomes familiar with his home waters, he will know where he is at any time by recognizing such structures as church steeples, water tanks, smokestacks, and unusual buildings. The sound signals all sailors become familiar with include bell, gong, and whistle buoys, and horns installed on lighthouses. A sounding is a measurement of the depth of the water. Soundings are taken to make sure there is enough water to keep the boat afloat, but also to help determine position. When a series of soundings is matched to a chart, it gives a rough approximation of position.

CHARTS

A chart is a nautical "road map." It is easily the most important aid to navigation available to the sailor. With a chart, he can determine where he is and what the waters hold. Without one, he might as well be blind, for he has no clue to what lies below the surface of the water. Charts of the coastal waters of the United States are published by the U. S. Coast and Geodetic Survey and distributed by the Coast Guard. Charts of the Great Lakes and the Mississippi River are produced by the U. S. Army Corps of Engineers.

The illustration shows a small portion of a typical chart. There isn't room here to describe everything shown on charts, but we can point out a few of the more important features. The numbers shown offshore in various positions indicate the depth of the water at mean low tide. The diamond-shaped symbols next to small dots represent buoys. The solid, heavy dots represent navigational lights. For example, the lighted buoy just east of the southern tip of Deer Island is a flashing red (FL R) light. There's a good deal more to charts than this very brief introduction. When you begin sailing, you should make it a point to become thoroughly familiar with the charts covering the waters you plan to use. You wouldn't think of making a long auto trip through strange country without a road map. Be just as sensible about sailing, and always have and use the chart covering the waters you are cruising.

Another very important feature of all charts is the *compass rose*. As the drawing shows, the compass rose consists of two circles, each

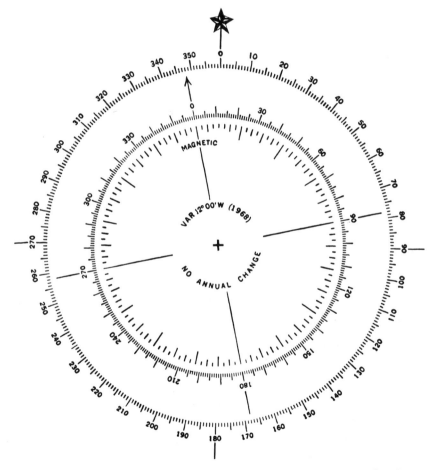

A typical compass rose, as seen on a chart. The inner circle shows magnetic north; these are the bearings that correspond to the readings of the boat's actual compass when there is no deviation.

calibrated into 360 degrees. The outer circle indicates *true north,* while the inner circle shows the direction of *magnetic north.* At the center of the compass rose the *variation* is shown, as well as how much it changes annually. Variation is simply the difference between true north and magnetic north for a given area.

It's important to understand the difference between true north and magnetic north, for the compass on your boat points to magnetic north, not true north. Of course, if there are some objects containing iron near the boat's compass, its reading will be affected. This effect is called *deviation.* Correcting for deviation is important for pinpoint navigation, but it need not concern you if you make sure no tools, machinery, or a radio are stored near the compass. In practice, the sailor looks at the magnetic circle of the compass rose to determine the course he must sail to reach a given destination, and then steers accordingly, using the boat's compass.

There is, of course, a great deal more to the use of charts than we have described here. Mastering the use of a chart is a task requiring much study and attention to detail. It is worth the effort, however, for someday a quick and accurate reading of a chart may save you from running onto a pile of rocks or aground on a sandbar.

BUOYS

In general, two types of buoys are in use on U.S. waters: unlighted buoys without sounds, and buoys that have sound and/or light. Buoys are used in a systematic way that makes it very clear to a sailor where he should steer his boat. This system is based on color, buoy shape, and numbering.

Imagine you are entering a channel or harbor from seaward. As you proceed up the channel, you will note that the buoys on the right-hand side are red; they are also marked with even numbers. The use of *red* for buoys on the *right* of a channel has given rise to a simple memory device: think *Red, Right, Returning* and you will always remember to leave the red buoys to starboard as you enter a channel, harbor, or river from seaward. Of course, when you are going toward the sea you would leave the red buoys to port.

The left-hand side of a channel is marked by black buoys with odd numbers. Buoy shape also distinguishes the right from the left side of a channel. The red buoys on the right are conical in shape; they are called *nun* buoys. The black buoys on the left are cylindrical;

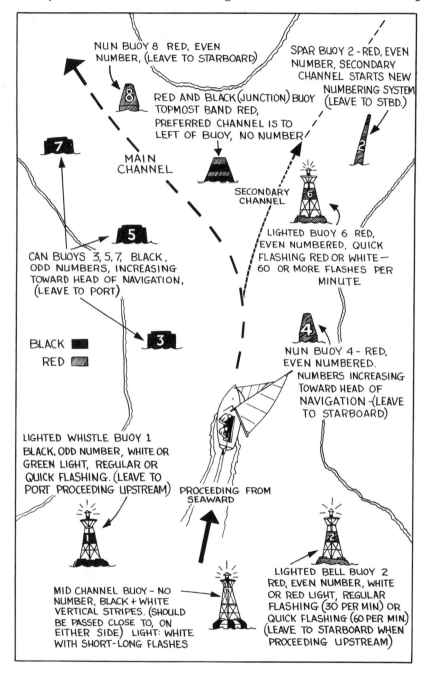

The buoyage system used on U.S. waters. Once you have learned the significance of the color, the shape, and the numbers used on buoys, finding your way is a relatively simple task.

they are called *can* buoys. Two other color schemes are in use. In one, black-and-white vertical stripes on an unnumbered buoy mark the middle of a channel. Boats should pass close by, but on either side of this type of buoy. In the other color scheme, black-and-red horizontal bands on a buoy indicate a channel junction or some type of underwater obstruction inside the channel itself. These buoys should be given a wide berth. They may be passed on either side, but the color of the top band indicates the preferred channel. In the drawing, for example, the red-and-black junction buoy's top band is red. Thus the preferred channel is to the left of the buoy; the boat leaves the red top to its starboard.

Buoys that have special importance to the navigator are lighted, equipped with sound, or both. Such buoys mark the entrance to a harbor; they are also used to mark a bend in a channel. To get some idea of the importance of light and sound in buoys, just consider the following situations. You are sailing on open water at night, and want to enter a sheltered harbor. As you approach land its mass is solid black to the eye. No landmarks are discernible. The entrance to the harbor, however, is marked by two lighted buoys. The one on the right will have either a red or a white light, with regular or quick flashing. The buoy on the left will have either a green or white light, again with regular or quick flashing. Your chart will tell you the color of the lights and also the nature of the flashing. Your job is to spot the buoys, and then sail cautiously between them to enter the harbor.

In the second situation, suppose you are caught in fog, but know

UNLIGHTED WHISTLE   LIGHTED GONG   UNLIGHTED BELL

Three additional types of buoys that you may encounter.

the general direction toward a sheltered harbor you wish to enter. Reference to your chart will tell you immediately if the harbor entrance is marked by bell or whistle buoys. With this information, you should proceed very cautiously toward the harbor entrance, following the sound of the buoys. Go very slowly and with great care in fog. You must be alert constantly to the possibility of collision. In addition, because sound behaves very strangely in fog, you must be alert to the possibility of straying away from the center of the harbor entrance.

One final comment about buoys is necessary. Every effort is made to maintain buoys in good condition and in their proper positions. This does not mean, however, that they will always be correctly placed. They may be adrift, off their charted positions due to heavy storms, unusual tides, and collisions, or even missing entirely. Because of these possibilities, a reasonable distance should always be allowed between the boat and a buoy when the buoy is passed.

THE COMPASS

If your sailing will never take you out of sight of familiar landmarks, you can probably do without a compass. On the other hand, if you plan to sail on large lakes, bays, or sounds, a good compass is a must. The compass should be mounted securely for easy reading by the helmsman, and away from large, iron-containing objects and electrical equipment. Always check before going out to make sure no iron or steel objects are near the compass. More than once I have discovered a sack of tools near the compass. The tools were placed there temporarily, but then forgotten. The deviation produced by such objects can greatly affect the compass reading.

Each compass has a line on its outside ring called the *lubberline.* This line indicates the heading of the boat; thus the compass must be mounted so that the lubberline and the centerline of the boat are parallel or coincide. When the compass has been installed in this position, the helmsman knows that the boat is headed in exactly the same direction as the compass reads. Of course, as you recall, this is the magnetic course, not the true course, which is represented by the outer ring of the compass rose.

If you are really interested in mastering the art of coastwise piloting, several other aids to navigation become necessary. These include (a) *dividers,* for measuring distance on the chart; (b) *parallel rules,* for plotting and moving a course on a chart to the nearest compass rose;

(c) a *lead line*, a weighted line used to measure the depth of the water; (d) *Coast Pilots*, books that give complete descriptions of ports, harbors, and coastlines; (e) *tide and current tables and charts*, and (f) *light and buoy lists*. Finally, a small *radio direction finder* (RDF) is a must if you expect to sail out of sight of land. An RDF allows you to get radio bearings—that is, the direction of a radio beacon or standard broadcast station from the boat. If you know the location on a chart of two or more sending stations, getting these bearings permits you to plot your position. An RDF is an indispensable aid in fog.

THE BUGEYE KETCH

The bugeye ketch is a large working sailboat developed during the latter part of the nineteenth century. As on all ketch-rigged boats, the mizzenmast is stepped forward of the tiller. *Little Jennie*, shown here, is said to be the oldest sailing yacht afloat. This boat was built in 1884, and later converted for pleasure use. *Jennie* is sixty-one feet long and carries the typical bugeye rig, with jib-headed sails and raked masts. The bugeye is an outgrowth of the Chesapeake Bay log canoe. Originally, bugeye ketches had a double-ended hull with a log bottom. Later they were built with conventional planking and framing. Surprising as it may seem in such a large boat, the bugeye carries a large centerboard, reflecting its earlier use as a working boat in shoal waters. (Photo by Peter Barlow)

16. Safety and Courtesy Afloat

Whenever we read or hear of a tragic accident that has taken place on the water, there is a tendency to think that it can't happen to us. Nothing could be farther from the truth. Accidents show no preference, unless it is to the habitually careless sailor. The careful sailor, on the other hand, can look forward to happy and rewarding hours on the water because he has made it a habit to prevent potential accidents before they have a chance to develop. This is the crux of the matter. Sailing, like other active sports, is not completely free of danger. It is, however, a sport whose dangerous elements can be controlled. The secret is to anticipate what might happen and then take preventive steps. This doesn't mean that you should be overly cautious. It does mean, however, that you should understand the capabilities of your boat, the sea and weather conditions you can expect to face, and yourself.

SAFETY EQUIPMENT

Throughout this book we have stressed safe sailing practices as well as the equipment needed to assure safety. At this point we want to bring the question of safety to a focus and review the essential equipment for a small sailboat. Keep in mind that the Coast Guard does not require all of the items we will list. Its requirements are the legal limits only. The prudent sailor will supplement the required equipment with enough additional equipment to handle whatever conditions the boat and crew can expect to meet.

To begin with, all boats should carry at least one Coast Guard approved life preserver for each person on board. Moreover, all persons on the boat should be instructed in the use of life preservers. At least one adequately heavy anchor plus enough anchor line is also a must. Be sure to include a bilge pump or bucket for bailing; you never know when your boat may leak, ship water from spray or high waves, or capsize. A sponge or absorbent rag is handy for completely drying the bilge. Be sure to carry some means of propulsion other than the sails. A pair of paddles or a small outboard engine is usually adequate for the small sailboat.

It's also wise to carry some tools and spare parts when you go out sailing. A good knife, a pair of pliers, and a screwdriver are essential. Also take along extra shackles, blocks, screws, and whatever other fittings you can't get along without. Would you be prepared if one of your sails were to tear? Probably not. Take along a sewing kit, as well as some of the newer tape for repairing sail rips, and this problem won't strand you in some strange place away from home port.

You should always carry a horn or whistle, adequate docking lines, a chart of the waters you are cruising, and a compass. Despite the fact that you may never use it, a first-aid kit is essential. Remember, however, to replace and refresh the contents of the first-aid kit periodically. Carry a flashlight at all times. You never know when you'll be delayed and have to make it into home port after dark. Of course, if you intend to sail at night, full navigation lights are required. Finally, carry extra line, a boathook, fenders, waterproof tape for quick repairs, and a small can of lubricating oil.

Be sure you understand the type of flotation used on your boat, if in fact it carries any flotation at all. Aluminum and fiberglass boats will sink if they are flooded, unless flotation has been installed. Wood centerboard boats will usually float when swamped, although wood keel boats will not. As the drawing shows, flotation tanks can be placed so that the boat will float either high or low when swamped. Low flotation tanks will often keep the water level below the top of the centerboard well, but the boat will be somewhat unstable; it may turn turtle when capsized. When the flotation tanks are placed high, the boat rides very low in the water. As a result, it is more stable, although the water level may be above the top of the centerboard well.

MAN OVERBOARD!

Despite every effort to prevent it from happening, people do fall or are knocked off sailboats. In calm weather, this is seldom a problem. It can be a serious problem in rough weather, however, for a sailboat is difficult to maneuver quickly and may injure the person in the water. There is a definite procedure to follow when someone falls off your boat. Learn it thoroughly, and you will save yourself a lot of trouble when you have to pick somebody out of the water. The first thing to do when somebody goes overboard is to make sure he has a life jacket. If he isn't wearing one, throw him one immediately. Next, have a member of the crew get the person overboard in his sight; *until the pickup, he should not take his eyes off the victim,* regardless of the maneuvering necessary to bring the boat alongside.

Getting the boat back to the person in the water may be a problem, especially if it is windy and high seas are running. If the accident oc-

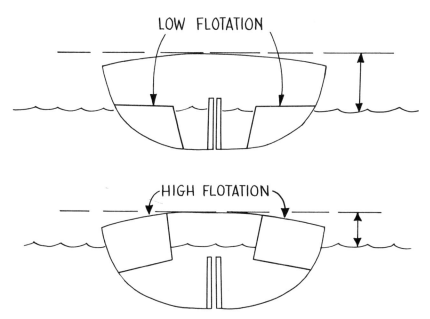

As these diagrams indicate, high flotation, while more stable than low flotation, may allow the water to rise above the top of the centerboard well when the boat is swamped. When the flotation is low, however, the water level may be below the top of the centerboard well, making it much easier to bail out the boat.

curred while you were running before the wind, you have two choices. You can bring the wind abeam, sail away for several boat lengths, come about, and sail back to the windward side of the victim. Or you can continue sailing before the wind for a short distance and then tack back to the person in the water. In either case, bring the boat to a stop in the water to windward of the victim, so that he is in the lee formed by the boat.

The preferred maneuver from tacks other than running before the wind is to jibe immediately so that you get back to the person in the water as quickly as possible. The drawing shows how this is done when the accident occurs with the boat on a beam reach. Some experts will tell you that even if jibing is a bit risky because of the wind, you should take the chance in order to get back to the victim as quickly as possible. However you choose to maneuver the boat back to the person in the water, stay far enough away during the pickup so that the hull cannot strike him. In very rough weather, try to get a line to the victim rather than attempt to have him catch hold of a heaving hull. To a person in the water, a violently heaving boat can be a lethal weapon.

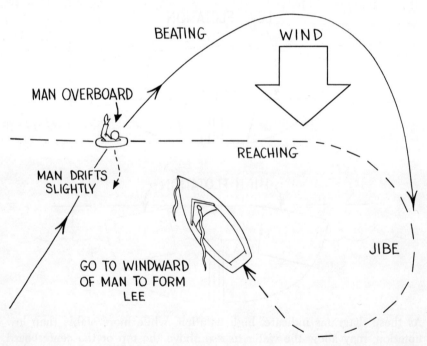

The quickest method for getting back to a man overboard is to jibe and then luff up to his windward.

If it should be your misfortune to go overboard someday, the first thing to do is keep calm. Stay afloat the easiest way you can—put on or hang on to the life jacket thrown to you. Don't tire yourself by trying to swim to the boat. Let it come to you. As it approaches, watch carefully, and if it appears to be coming too close, use your strength to swim clear. Then, after you have caught hold of the gunwale of the boat, or a line, climb back aboard over the stern. Dry yourself quickly, and put on warm clothes to avoid catching cold.

DISTRESS SIGNALS

Like it or not, every sailor someday faces the prospect of an equipment breakdown. The problem may be a sail tear too large for temporary repair, a broken rudder or tiller, or even a dismasting. In any event, the day will come when you will need help. In all probability, if you are in a small boat, you have to rely on some means of communication other than a radio to summon help. Many sailors erroneously think that all it takes is a shout or a wave of the arms to bring help. This just isn't so. Although most sailors stand ready to assist in an emergency (a tradition of the sea, by the way), they frequently misinterpret shouting and waving of the arms as friendly greetings, and pass by without stopping.

Sometimes, when sailors have no knowledge at all of the correct distress signals, it is purely a matter of luck that they obtain any help at all. In one instance that I recall, three young boys in a fourteen-foot sailboat were anchored in a strong rip tide about two hundred yards offshore. The time was near nightfall. The boys were just sitting in the boat, caught in the grip of an apathy that was immediately noticeable. Evidently they had exhausted themselves shouting and waving at passing boats, and finally could do nothing but sit and wait for help. When they were finally approached by a boat under power, they explained that they could not sail in against the rip tide, had become frightened, and then had anchored before trying to get help from a passing boat. But then, the people on every boat that went by simply waved back at them and continued on their way. If someone hadn't stopped to help, the boys would have been stranded after dark with no lights and no prospects for help.

There are several basic distress signals available to the small-boat sailor. These should be learned, and then used only in the event of

SOUND HORN, BELL,
OR WHISTLE RAPIDLY
AND REPEATEDLY

BLINK WHITE RANGE
LIGHT, OR A SPOTLIGHT, TO
SIGNAL S.O.S. IT'S 3 DOTS,
3 DASHES, 3 DOTS

REVERSE FLAG OR
ENSIGN SO THAT IT FLIES
UPSIDE DOWN

SLOWLY AND REPEATEDLY RAISE AND
LOWER BOTH ARMS OUTSTRETCHED AT
THE SIDES

The most useful distress signals for the small-boat sailor. Never give a distress signal unless you mean it.

distress. They should never be used in jest. The drawing shows what to do. If you have no signaling equipment on board, stand up and "slowly and repeatedly raise and lower both arms outstretched at the sides." This is a universally recognized distress signal and should bring help in quick order. If you have a horn or a whistle on board, try sounding it in repeated short blasts. At night, you can blink a light in the time-honored S-O-S sequence; this is three short flashes, three long flashes, and three short flashes (..., – – –, ...). Finally, if you carry the ensign (the American flag) on board, you can fly it upside down to indicate that your boat is in distress. A radar reflector is another useful signal for boats that sometimes find themselves caught in fog. Inexpensive foldup versions are available. Such a reflector is most useful on small wood and fiberglass boats, for these small vessels show up very poorly, if at all, on radar screens. A reflector run up to the masthead on a halyard, however, appears as a bright blip on radar screens.

OVERLOADING

Many inexperienced boatmen make the mistake of overloading their boats. The wise skipper will determine ahead of time just how many people and how much weight constitute a safe load for his boat. He will then plan his cruises so that he is never overloaded. It is difficult to turn people away when they expect to go sailing. Thus it is important to carefully control the number of people who come aboard.

It is essential that every skipper know the capacity of his boat. Many new boats carry a plate showing this capacity in *number of persons* and in *total load weight,* including persons, engine, fuel, and all loose gear. It is also important to make your passengers understand that moving about on a small boat has a marked effect on the boat's stability. Always remember to distribute the load evenly and to keep it low in the boat except when the crew is hiking out. Under ordinary circumstances, the crew should not stand up and move about. This not only affects the boat's stability, it also interferes with the boat's trim, an important factor in sailing.

For the most part, sailors avoid overloading their boats. Occasionally, however, you will see a small sailboat with six or more youngsters crowded into the cockpit and sprawled out on the foredeck. It looks as if everyone is having a wonderful time, although the boat in such situations always seems on the brink of swamping or capsizing. One can't help but wonder if everyone on board can swim, and if there are enough life jackets for all hands. All too often one or more of these youngsters cannot swim well enough to take care of himself in the event of a capsize, and a senseless drowning results.

DROWNPROOFING

The great majority of drownings associated with boating accidents need not occur. Too often sailors thrown into the water forget or refuse to stay with the boat. In addition, many have never attempted to learn how to stay afloat fully clothed, or even how to disrobe in the water. These are important, of course, because sailors often wear bulky clothes to guard against the elements.

Drownproofing is a technique of floating that all sailors should know. It is particularly valuable, for it allows the person in the water to remain afloat for long periods of time with little or no energy expended. Moreover, it is a technique that can be quite successfully carried out even when fully clothed. If you are not a reasonably good swimmer, you should never sail without wearing a life jacket. In addition, you should not attempt to learn this drownproofing technique unless you are a good swimmer, and under no circumstances should you attempt to learn it alone. Work with another competent swimmer, and practice by the side of a pool or close to the edge of a dock. Wear just a bathing suit at first. If you have any doubt about your swimming ability, seek professional help from a Red Cross or YMCA water safety instructor.

As the drawing shows, the floating or resting position, also called the front survival position, consists of the body being erect in the water, with the waist slightly flexed and the face tipped forward; the hands and arms dangle in a relaxed fashion. The breath is held in this position for four or five seconds. At this point, in order to raise the head above water for a breath of air, the arms and legs are used to propel the body upward. The hands are forced downward accompanied by a scissor kick. This lifts the body sufficiently for an inhalation. During the motion upward, while the face is still submerged, a full exhalation takes place through the nose. If this is done correctly, the head needs to be out of the water only long enough for an inhalation. After taking the fresh breath of air, the head is tipped forward again, and the body is allowed to return to the original floating position. Rhythm is very important. Once an easy, smooth cycle has been mastered, the swimmer can float this way for very long periods of time indeed.

The technique of "drownproofing" takes advantage of the fact that with very few exceptions the body will float vertically when the lungs are fully inflated. See the text for details.

Mastering this skill will teach you a great deal about what type of clothing to wear while sailing. As you practice with clothing on, you will discover that lightweight clothing that allows maximum movement is the best. We hope that you will never have to use this technique in seriousness. We also hope that should you find yourself in the water with a capsized boat, you will be able to stay with it and wait for help. On the other hand, the day may come when you are in the water separated from your boat. Your chances for survival will be much greater if you have made yourself "drownproof."

FLAG ETIQUETTE

Several different flags may be flown from sailboats, but strict tradition dictates where they are flown and under what conditions. There isn't room here to describe the proper use of all of these flags, such as the crew's meal flag, the absent flag, and the guest flag. Instead, we will indicate the proper use of just three flags: the yacht ensign, the burgee (pennant) of the owner's yacht club, and the owner's private flag. An important point to remember is that a flag identifies a boat and its owner with an organization or group. Thus the owner is responsible at all times that the flag is in full view for conduct that reflects favorably on the organization. This rule is most important in the case of the yacht ensign. This is our country's flag; while it is being flown, whoever is handling the boat should conduct himself in a manner that is completely above reproach.

The yacht ensign may be flown two ways aboard a sailboat. When the boat is at anchor, or when it is under power, the ensign is flown on a staff at the stern. When the boat is under sail, the ensign is flown from the leech of a jib-headed mainsail, about a third of the way down from the top. On a gaff-rigged boat, the ensign is flown at the peak. The greatest temptation, and the error most often seen, is to fly the ensign from the stern even when the boat is under sail. Certainly no harm is done when a flag is flown incorrectly, but tradition is important and should be honored. After all, by honoring these customs every sailor shows his pride in the United States as a great seafaring nation.

The owner's private signal and the club burgee are flown at the masthead, but not at the same time. The owner's signal is flown only when the boat is under way. When the boat is anchored or moored, the owner's signal is hauled down and the yacht club burgee goes up in its place.

COURTESY AFLOAT

All sailors have equal rights and privileges when on the water. By the same token, however, all sailors carry the responsibility to respect the rights of their fellow boatmen. This means much more than obeying the rules of the road to the letter. It involves anticipating the desires and movements of the other skipper's boat and then taking action to respect his rights.

In order to cover as many courtesy situations as possible, we will list them as a series of DO's and DON'Ts. This will give you a quick reference for courtesy problems, and permit us to make the best use of available space.

DO stay clear of boats that are racing. If you must sail through a racing fleet, DO pass astern of all boats sailing closehauled, and DO keep to leeward of all boats running free.

DO go to the help of fellow boatmen in distress. This is a universal obligation. Always remember that tomorrow you may need help.

DON'T assume that because you belong to a yacht club, all other clubs will automatically extend full privileges to you. When approaching a strange club the first time, ask the attendant what privileges you are entitled to.

DON'T go aboard another boat until you are invited by the owner. It is considered a grave breach of etiquette to board a boat without an invitation.

DO be courteous and friendly to people in the unfamiliar harbors you visit. You will find that an outgoing, friendly manner will be received most cordially in most harbors.

DO anchor clear of channels and traffic lanes in strange anchorages. In addition, DON'T drop your anchor over another anchor line unless an emergency forces you to do so.

DON'T be a litterbug. DO save your garbage and trash in suitable containers until you can dispose of it ashore.

DON'T play a radio or phonograph late into the night in a crowded harbor. Many cruising sailors go to bed with the sunset and get up with the sunrise.

DON'T butt in with unasked-for advice while aboard someone else's boat. Follow the wishes of the skipper while you are his guest. He expects to behave the same way aboard your boat.

DON'T abuse your right-of-way privilege over powerboats. As pointed out earlier, it is the better part of valor to give way in any situation that might endanger or otherwise inconvenience the powerboat skipper.

DO learn to recognize the skindiver's flag and stay clear of skindiving activities. The flag is bright red-orange with a diagonal white stripe.

DON'T tie up to government navigation buoys, or land at a private dock or float except in an emergency. The law forbids anyone to tie up at a navigation aid maintained or authorized by the Coast Guard, so think twice before tying up at a buoy, even in an emergency.

17. Caring for Your Boat

Although this is the last chapter of *The Complete Beginner's Guide to Sailing*, it is by no means the least important. Just as the sheer fun of sailing is partially counterbalanced by the inevitable element of danger, the enjoyment of well-maintained equipment is offset by the need for year-round maintenance. There is no escaping it. The elements and hard use combine to take a heavy toll on paint, varnish, gel coat, rigging, and sails unless continual efforts are made to keep a craft in top shape.

There are two aspects to caring for your sailboat. One has to do with where you will keep it. Many small-boat owners trailer their boats, while others use the facilities of a yacht club, marina, or boatyard. Despite the fact that some sailors may not be old enough to drive a car, we will discuss trailering in some detail. What we have to say will come in handy later, when today's young readers are driving. The other aspect of caring for your boat has to do with maintenance. As you will discover, this is a year-round chore. There is no need, however, to look at maintenance with any sense of foreboding. When the necessary up-keep chores on a boat are performed in a routine manner the year round, these responsibilities become a natural but not burdensome part of boating. Of course, if your boat is an old "clunker," you may find maintenance occupying all of your time and effort, to the exclusion of any sailing fun.

As pointed out earlier, modern methods of construction using the most up-to-date materials have given us durable and relatively easy-to-maintain hulls, rigging, and sails. Hulls of fiberglass and aluminum, stainless steel rigging, aluminum spars, and sails of Dacron and nylon are relatively maintenance-free. Nylon and Dacron lines have replaced manila lines, also reducing the cost of operating a boat. Finally, modern antifouling paints keep a boat's bottom relatively clean compared with the situation just a few years ago.

TRAILERING

One of the great advantages of owning a small sailboat, especially a centerboarder, is that it need not be moored in a permanent anchorage or berthed in a slip. Instead, it can be stored anywhere you like on a trailer. Another advantage is that virtually all bodies of water that have launching ramps are available for sailing fun. Small boats kept in the water, on the other hand, are confined to the immediate area of home port.

Selecting a trailer for a boat requires careful thought. The trailer should provide support in the right places, so that the hull will not sag and lose its shape. With respect to the size of the trailer, follow this rule of thumb: Take the total weight of the boat fully equipped; if this figure is within one hundred pounds of the rated capacity of a trailer, choose the next larger trailer. A well-designed trailer will meet all local and state regulations and will provide good riding comfort with maximum safety in the towing car. Of great importance, dry launching with a minimum of physical effort should be possible. If you are in doubt, consult a dealer who is familiar with the different types of trailers and what they are designed to do. Buying a trailer is somewhat like buying tires; safety and reliability depend on quality.

Load distribution is an important factor in how well a boat on a trailer will ride. In general, the boat's center of gravity should be a bit forward of the trailer wheels. This will produce sufficient weight at the tongue of the trailer—something in excess of one hundred pounds. Take care to adjust this bumper-weight figure. If tongue weight is too great, the rear of the car will be forced down. If it is too little, the trailer will bob up and down at the rear bumper and produce a very uneven and unsafe ride. It's quite simple to shift the center of gravity of a boat on a trailer. Simply move the contents of the boat forward or aft to obtain a better balance.

A number of special precautionary measures when driving are neces-

THE CAT BOAT

Cat boats are believed to have descended from the old centerboard sloops used by pre-Civil War fishermen. The boat shown here is a Crosby "cat"; it was built between 1910 and 1920. This boat is typical of the type that became popular in the Nantucket, Martha's Vineyard, and Cape Cod area during the late 1800s. At one time cat boats were the most common single-masted sailboats in the New England region. Cat boats have a wide beam, a spacious cabin, a strong centerboard, and a large and deep rudder. Their powerful hull form is extremely seaworthy. They are shallow-draft boats, and thus sail well in shoal waters. Today cat boats are enjoying a new popularity, for sailors are discovering their good sailing characteristics, their spaciousness, and their ease of handling. (Photo by Peter Barlow)

sary with a trailer following behind. First, check the trailer regulations to make sure your rig complies for all of the states within which you plan to travel. For example, you will probably need a rear light that includes a brake signal and directional signals, and you may need brakes on the trailer itself. Launch only at approved hard-surfaced ramps to avoid getting your trailer and car stuck in sand or mud. When on the road, remember that you are carrying an extra-heavy load and that a much greater stopping distance is required. Also remember to swing wide when passing and to allow extra room up ahead.

Most drivers experience their greatest difficulty when backing a trailer. Some practice is needed, of course, but if you remember to turn the steering wheel opposite to the direction in which you want the rear of the trailer to turn, you should minimize this difficulty. For example, to turn the rear of the trailer to the left, the steering wheel is turned to the right. Try it, but practice in a light traffic area before attempting to launch a boat.

There are certain steps to follow when launching a small sailboat from a trailer. First, step the mast and fasten the stays and shrouds. Make sure that the mast is positioned properly. Next, attach the boom and the running rigging. Finally, bend on the sails, but do not raise them until after the boat is in the water. To launch the boat, bring the trailer to the water at right angles to the shoreline, and be careful not to back down too far. There is nothing more embarrassing than a half-sunk stalled car and trailer.

Once the boat is in the water, getting away may still be a bit of a problem. It will be necessary to hoist the sails and get the boat into water deep enough for the centerboard and rudder. The wind, of course, is a factor in getting away successfully. If the wind is onshore, that is, blowing in toward the shore, the problem is to get the boat into deep enough water to beat away from shore. The crew should go aboard first, raise the sails, and then prepare the rudder and centerboard for dropping into position. The skipper (or helmsman) then positions himself at the stern of the boat, wades out a few feet, and pushes the boat out into deeper water as he climbs aboard over the transom. The crew can assist in getting the boat into deeper water by paddling. Once aboard, the skipper drops the rudder in place and the crew lowers the centerboard when the water is deep enough. If the boat is angled correctly to sail away on a beat, it is only necessary to sheet in the sails. If the boat is pointed directly into the wind, however, it will be necessary to back the jib to fall off on the desired tack.

The task is somewhat easier if the wind is blowing offshore or parallel to the shoreline. In this case, the skipper should get aboard while the crew holds the boat in place with its bow pointed in toward shore. The skipper raises the sails and fastens the rudder in position. The sheet lines are left free. Then, with the skipper balancing the boat and holding the rudder amidships, the crew pushes off and climbs aboard. As the boat backs out into the water, the skipper turns the rudder to bring the bow around. As the boat slows and turns, the sheets are drawn in. Just as the boat stops backing, the tiller is reversed to sail the boat away from shore, and the centerboard is dropped about halfway down. Once the boat is in deep enough water, the centerboard is lowered all the way. A somewhat less seamanlike technique is simply to paddle the boat out into deep enough water before raising the sails, lowering the centerboard, and attaching the rudder and tiller. If you elect to do this, be sure to point the bow into the wind before raising the sails, mainsail first.

YACHT CLUB, MARINA, OR BOATYARD?

The boat owner has a choice of summer accommodations for his boat. He may elect to trailer his craft and store it in the backyard between outings. This is one of the least expensive ways to enjoy sailing, but it does involve learning to handle a trailer rig. Other choices include a yacht club, a marina, or a boatyard. Whichever you choose, however, there are just a few ways to tie up and store a boat. The most convenient, and often the most expensive, is the *floating dock*. These ride up and down with the tide and provide a finger next to the boat from which it is boarded quite easily. A less expensive choice is a *slip* between pilings. A boat in such a slip rides up and down with the tide, requiring that care be taken when docking lines are put out, for the pilings and any walks constructed on them are immovable. As a result, tying up and getting on and off a boat may be difficult at low tide.

For the majority of boat owners, the *offshore mooring* is the most attractive way to keep a boat in the water. A sound mooring, which should be designed for local conditions, is lower in cost than a trailer. To learn the best mooring rig for local conditions, consult the harbor master, dock master of the yacht club, or proprietor of the marina or boatyard. In many localities you may choose an open spot and put down your own mooring. If you do this, of course, maintenance of the mooring is your own responsibility. You will need to make arrangements to put the mooring in at the beginning of the season and take it out at the end of the season. Moorings maintained by yacht clubs, marinas, or boatyards, and sometimes by coastal towns, however, are rented out by the season. These range in cost from the very modestly priced town moorings to the very expensive yacht club and marina moorings with launch and other special services.

There isn't room here to describe in detail the different services offered by yacht clubs, marinas, and boatyards. We can, however, give you a brief description of the various services and encourage you to investigate thoroughly before you make a decision. Boating pleasure depends upon a happy frame of mind. If you are dissatisfied in any way with the service you are receiving from your club, marina, or boatyard, the chances are that the hours spent aboard your boat will be somewhat less than completely gratifying.

Yacht clubs range in size and services from the small club devoted exclusively to sailing activities, to large and elaborate organizations that offer year-round social and recreational activities. In some of these larger organizations, boating has become a secondary activity. There is probably no such thing as the typical yacht club. If one did exist, however, it would probably offer instruction in sailing, seamanship, swimming, and safety. It would also conduct a full summer calendar of races and cruises, and perhaps two or three major summer social affairs.

The marina is a relatively new development in boating services. In many ways, the marina is a cross between the yacht club and boatyard. It offers those services of both that are in greatest demand by the boating public. It might be said that the marina is a commercial yacht club. Services that can be expected are a mooring or a slip; a clean and well-laid-out dock and parking area; a gasoline dock; some repair and maintenance services, including outdoor winter storage, the capacity to launch and take out fairly large boats, a clubhouse-type building often containing a snack bar, toilet and shower facilities, a marine stores shop, lockers, and other facilities; and finally, attendants and watchmen to police the entire area. Some marinas are excellent, but others are little more than boating slums. Thus care is required when a marina is selected.

The boatyard represents the most primitive commercially run home for your boat. You can expect crude docking and mooring facilities, lockers in some but not all boatyards, and occasionally toilet and shower facilities. Boatyards generally do not offer launch service, but there may be one or two old rowboats available for getting out to moored boats. A plus for boatyards is repair and maintenance service. This is the real reason for the boatyard's existence, so you can expect these services to be good. Many boatyards rent space for winter storage and will permit a certain amount of do-it-yourself work on a boat. Many marinas also permit do-it-yourself activities, but both usually require that you purchase tools and supplies through the yard and not elsewhere. In addition, you will probably not be permitted to bring in outside labor to work on your boat.

SPRING CARE

After the long winter storage period, either indoors or outside, a boat requires certain work before it can be put in the water. If you have performed all of the necessary fall lay-up chores conscientiously, getting your boat back on the water is an invigorating and satisfying activity. If you neglected those fall tasks, however, you will probably be late getting back on the water, and lose a lot of sailing enjoyment. If the boat is to remain in the water all season long, it will be necessary to coat the bottom with antifouling paint. There are several different types of antifouling paint, as well as different formulas for salt and fresh water. The best procedure is to inquire about the most effective type of paint for your area. As you will discover, some paints seem to perform better than others. Of course, if you plan to trailer your boat, antifouling paint is not necessary, for the boat will probably not be in the water long enough for any bottom growth to develop. There isn't room here to discuss other painting tasks you may face. The hull or topside of the boat, for example, may require painting. If this is the case, it would be wise to consult a local marine-paint dealer for the best paint available.

Another necessary spring chore is varnishing the *brightwork*. You will discover that much of the varnished woodwork on the boat will need a new coat or two every year. Sand the old coat down with fine sandpaper before applying the new coat. If the old varnish is checked or otherwise broken, consult the instructions on the varnish can for preparing the surface.

Another important spring chore is a complete inspection of all fittings and rigging. Be particularly sure that all fittings that handle line, such as fairleads and cleats, are tight. Tighten those that have loosened.

Clean all metal, and polish it to protect against the elements. Make a particularly close inspection of the tiller and rudder assembly. Look for excessive wear, and check to be sure the rudder hasn't warped. Thoroughly clean the interior of the boat, and return all loose gear that you removed at fall lay-up time. Finally, run through a checklist of required and extra safety gear, and repair or replace wherever necessary.

If your boat has aluminum spars, it will be necessary to clean them with an abrasive substance and then apply polish or wax. Aluminum oxidizes, and over the winter will collect a layer of oxide scale. Anodized aluminum, on the other hand, does not need to be scrubbed down with an abrasive. It only requires a good washing before application of a protective coating of wax. A good-quality automobile wax does a very satisfactory job. A final chore on the mast is inspection of all rigging and fittings. In particular, carefully examine the halyards for wear. If any wear is evident, it is probably a good idea to replace the halyard rather than take a chance on it.

MIDSEASON CARE

Care for your boat does not end once it has been launched. Throughout the sailing season, there are a number of inspection and maintenance chores you should carry out routinely. The running rigging, for example, should be inspected for wear each time you go out sailing. In addition, make periodic checks of all standing rigging. Pay particular attention to wire rigging, especially where the wire passes over pulleys or sheaves.

If you are going to race your boat, its bottom will need periodic cleaning. This is especially true if the boat is left in the water all season long. Even the best antifouling paints will not prevent the growth of marine or aquatic slimes. As a result, it will be necessary to haul the boat out for a good scrub every month or six weeks. Another way to do it is to bring the boat in close to shore and then go into the water to scrub down the bottom. This takes a good swimmer, for it is necessary to take a deep breath and duck under while scrubbing. I remember doing this as a youngster in Maine waters. Believe me, we scrubbed all the harder because the water was so cold!

Sails also require care; if you recall, we discussed this earlier in the book. It might be wise, however, to remind you of one or two maintenance tips on Dacron. This synthetic material should be kept clean of oil or grease. Use a spot remover such as carbon tetrachloride to remove any oil or grease spots, but be sure to work in a well-ventilated area. In addition, try to remember to keep extreme heat away from Dacron, and avoid sharp creases in the material.

If you think of your boat as a structure that requires maintaining, it becomes easier to attend to the routine inspections needed to keep the craft in top condition. Actually, little more than a watchful eye is required, followed up immediately with service or repair, to keep your boat in top condition. But it is necessary to "think maintenance"; a sailboat will go downhill rapidly if it is not cared for. This is part of the fun of sailing, however. A skipper takes pride in his craft; thus he willingly assumes responsibility for its condition.

FALL CARE

Fall means the end of the boating season for most sailors. Of course, those who live in states such as Florida and California can enjoy sailing all year round. These sailors are to be envied by the rest of us who must lay up our boats for the long winter. Preparing a boat for winter storage consists of much more than just hauling it out and throwing a tarpaulin over the top. Certain chores must be performed if the boat is to get through the winter without damage, and if getting it back into the water the following spring is to be accomplished easily.

The first task following hauling is to scrub the bottom. This is most easily done immediately upon hauling, not the next day or some other later time. The growth that has accumulated on the bottom comes off easiest while still wet. Once it has had a chance to dry out, removal is extremely difficult. Many yards include scrubbing the bottom in the price of hauling the boat and setting it in its cradle for winter storage. This is all well and good, but you should go over the bottom yourself to make sure it is thoroughly clean. Very often areas of the hull are overlooked, and if the boat was taken out by means of a travel lift, the portions of the hull under the lifting straps were probably not scrubbed down.

After the boat has been placed in its cradle, check to be sure that the hull is supported at all of the proper spots. A hull out of the water is subject to many weight strains it does not experience in the water. While in the water, the hull is supported by water pressure at every point below the waterline. Too often hulls sag and seams part because boats were put up for winter storage quickly and carelessly.

All loose gear should be removed from the boat before putting on the winter cover. Be especially careful to remove items that may be affected by cold weather. Above all, do not leave any food aboard. It will just attract insects and mice, and also confront you with a messy situation when you pull off the winter cover the following spring.

Finally, do not neglect to care for your sails during the off season. Inspect them carefully, and if any repairs are necessary, get them to a nearby sailmaker for mending and washing as soon as possible. Many sailmakers also store sails during the winter. Don't wait until early spring to have your sails repaired. If you take them to a sailmaker during the fitting-out season, you may wait a long time before getting them back. Thus you could miss much of the fine early-season sailing that characterizes many U.S. waters.

Index

At the age of thirteen, "Lee" Drummond built his own fourteen-foot skiff, and he has been sailing now for over twenty years. He has taught sailing as well as swimming, life saving, canoeing, and boating, and has racing experience in the Lightning Class and in cruising class yachts. He was born in New York City and received his B.A. degree from Bowdoin College, an M.S. in Ed. and an M.A. from Hofstra University, and a C.A.S. degree from Wesleyan University. Mr. Drummond is editor-in-chief of the school department for a textbook publishing company, and lives in Lynnfield, Massachusetts with his wife, son, and daughter.

George O'Day, who wrote the Foreword to THE COMPLETE BEGINNER'S GUIDE TO SAILING, is the author of several sailing books and a frequent contributor to sailing publications such as *Popular Boating, Yachting, One-Design Yachtsman,* and *Rudder.* He won an Olympic Gold Medal in 1960 for sailing in the International 5.5 meter class, and crewed on the *Weatherly* and the *Intrepid,* both of which competed successfully in the America's Cup races.